PHP Development Tool Essentials

Chad Russell

Apress®

PHP Development Tool Essentials

Chad Russell
Jacksonville, Florida, USA

ISBN-13 (pbk): 978-1-4842-0684-3   ISBN-13 (electronic): 978-1-4842-0683-6
DOI 10.1007/978-1-4842-0683-6

Library of Congress Control Number: 2016947166

Managing Director: Welmoed Spahr
Lead Editor: Steve Anglin
Technical Reviewer: Massimo Nardone
Editorial Board: Steve Anglin, Pramila Balan, Laura Berendson, Aaron Black, Louise Corrigan, Jonathan Gennick, Robert Hutchinson, Celestin Suresh John, Nikhil Karkal, James Markham, Susan McDermott, Matthew Moodie, Natalie Pao, Gwenan Spearing
Coordinating Editor: Mark Powers
Copy Editor: April Rondeau
Compositor: SPi Global
Indexer: SPi Global
Artist: SPi Global

Distributed to the book trade worldwide by Springer Science+Business Media New York, 233 Spring Street, 6th Floor, New York, NY 10013. Phone 1-800-SPRINGER, fax (201) 348-4505, e-mail orders-ny@springer-sbm.com, or visit www.springeronline.com. Apress Media, LLC is a California LLC and the sole member (owner) is Springer Science + Business Media Finance Inc (SSBM Finance Inc). SSBM Finance Inc is a Delaware corporation.

For information on translations, please e-mail rights@apress.com, or visit www.apress.com.

Apress and friends of ED books may be purchased in bulk for academic, corporate, or promotional use. eBook versions and licenses are also available for most titles. For more information, reference our Special Bulk Sales–eBook Licensing web page at www.apress.com/bulk-sales.

Any source code or other supplementary materials referenced by the author in this text is available to readers at www.apress.com/9781484206843. For detailed information about how to locate your book's source code, go to www.apress.com/source-code/. Readers can also access source code at SpringerLink in the Supplementary Material section for each chapter.

Printed on acid-free paper

Contents at a Glance

Contents

About the Author

Chad Russell is the founder and chief technologist at Intuitive Reason, a firm that specializes in building web-based applications and ecommerce platforms for mid- to enterprise-size clients using open source solutions.

About the Technical Reviewer

Massimo Nardone holds a Master of Science degree in Computing Science from the University of Salerno, Italy. He has worked as a project manager, software engineer, research engineer, chief security architect, information security manager, PCI/SCADA auditor, and senior lead IT security/cloud/SCADA architect for many years. He currently works as the chief information security officer (CISO) for Cargotec Oyj. He has more than 22 years of work experience in IT, including in security, SCADA, cloud computing, IT infrastructure, mobile, security, and WWW technology areas for both national and international projects. He worked as a visiting lecturer and supervisor for exercises at the Networking Laboratory of the Helsinki University of Technology (Aalto University). He has been programming and teaching how to program with Android, Perl, PHP, Java, VB, Python, C/C++, and MySQL for more than 20 years. He holds four international patents (PKI, SIP, SAML, and Proxy areas). He is the coauthor of *Pro Android Games* (Apress, 2015).

CHAPTER 1

■ ■ ■

Version Control

If you're not already using some type of version control on your project, you should definitely start now. Whether you're a single developer or part of a bigger team, version control provides numerous benefits to any project, big or small.

If you're not familiar with what version control is, it is a system used to capture and record changes in files within your project. It provides you with a visual history of these changes, giving you the ability to go back and see who made the changes, what they changed–both files and the changed contents, when they made the change, and, by reading their commit message, why it was changed. In addition, it provides you with a mechanism to segregate changes in your code, called *branches* (more on that later).

There are a number of version control systems available, some free and open source, others proprietary and requiring licensing. For the purposes of this chapter, we'll be focusing on the free and open source Git. Git was first developed by Linus Torvalds for the Linux Kernel project. Git is a distributed version control system (DVCS) that allows you to distribute many copies (mirrors) of your repository to other members of your team so as to be able to track changes. This means that each person with a clone of the repository has an entire working copy of the system at the time of the clone. Git was built to be simple, fast, and fully distributable.

This chapter is meant to give you an overview of Git, covering enough information to get you started using it every day in your projects. Since I only have one chapter in which to cover this, I'll only touch on the surface of Git's most commonly used functionality. However, this should be more than enough to get you comfortable with using it. For a more complete, in-depth look at Git, check out *Pro Git* by Scott Chacon and Ben Straub, available from Apress.

Using Git

To start using Git, you first need to install it on your system. Binaries for Mac OS X, Windows, Linux, and Solaris are available by visiting http://git-scm.com and downloading the appropriate binary install for your OS. In addition to this, Git is also available for RedHat/CentOS systems using the yum package manager or apt-get on Debian/Ubuntu. On Mac OS X, you can get it by installing the Xcode command line tools. In this manuscript, we will use a Linux version of Git.

© Chad Russell 2016
C. Russell, *PHP Development Tool Essentials*, DOI 10.1007/978-1-4842-0683-6_1

Git Configuration

Now that Git is installed, let's do a minimum amount of configuration by setting your name and email address in the Git configuration tool so that this information will be shown for commits that you make (a *commit* being the act of placing a new version of your code in the repository). We can do this using the git config tool:

```
$ git config --global user.name "Chad Russell"
$ git config --global user.email chad@intuitivereason.com
```

We can verify that these settings took by using the git config tool again, this time using the property key as the setting we want to check:

```
$ git config user.name
Chad Russell
$ git config user.email
chad@intuitivereason.com
```

Notice that you will run the same configuration commands in both Windows and Unix environments.

Initializing Your Repository

To create your first Git repository, you will simply use the git init command. This will initialize an empty Git repository in your source code directory. Once you initialize, you can then perform your first commit to your new repository. For this example, we have an empty directory that we'll initialize in, then we will add a README file, and finally we'll add and commit the file to our new repository.

Remember that Git will initiate based on the directory in which the Git command will be called. For instance, if you are in

```
C:\Program Files (x86)\Git
```

then the result will be

```
Initialized empty Git repository in C:/Program Files (x86)/Git/bin/.git/
```

We'll use the following repository and directory as the book progresses to track various code examples that we'll use:

```
$ git init
Initialized empty Git repository in /Apress/source/.git/
```

Initial Commit

Now that we have initialized our empty repository, we'll add a very basic README file to it and then perform our initial commit:

```
$ echo "This is our README." > README.md
```

Now, if we look at the current status of our repository using git status we'll see that we now have one untracked file, meaning one file that isn't yet added to our repository or being tracked for changes by Git. You can use git status any time you'd like to view the status of the working branch of your repository:

```
$ git status
On branch master

Initial commit

Untracked files:
  (use "git add <file>..." to include in what will be committed)

        README.md
```

Now, we'll add the file to our repository using git add:

```
$ git add README.md
```

If we view the git status again, we'll see our file has been added, but not yet committed (saved) to the repository:

```
$ git status
On branch master

Initial commit

Changes to be committed:
  (use "git rm --cached <file>..." to unstage)

        new file:   README.md
```

Lastly, we'll commit our change, and our new README will now be in our repository and be tracked for changes going forward:

```
$ git commit -m "Initial commit. Added our README"
[master (root-commit) e504d64] Initial commit. Added our README
 1 file changed, 1 insertion(+)
 create mode 100644 README.md
```

We can see from the message we received back from git commit that our commit was saved. Now, if we check the git status one more time we'll see we currently have nothing else to commit:

```
$ git status
On branch master
nothing to commit, working directory clean
```

Staging Changes

We have our initial tracked file in our repository and have seen how to add a new file to Git to be tracked. Let's now change the README and then stage and commit this change.

I've added a change to the README.md file, altering the initial text we added to something slightly more informative. Let's run git status again and see what it shows:

```
$ git status
On branch master
Changes not staged for commit:
  (use "git add <file>..." to update what will be committed)
  (use "git checkout -- <file>..." to discard changes in working directory)

        modified:   README.md
```

It shows that our README was modified, but that it's not staged for commit yet. We do this by using the git add command. We'll add it and check the status one more time:

```
$ git add README.md
$ git status
On branch master
Changes to be committed:
  (use "git reset HEAD <file>..." to unstage)

        modified:   README.md
```

Lastly, we'll make this new commit, which will wrap up the change to the file we made:

```
$ git commit -m "Updated README"
[master ca476b6] Updated README
 1 file changed, 1 insertion(+), 1 deletion(-)
```

■ **Note**   The staging changes may be configured a bit differently in a Windows environment.

Viewing History

With all of the changes we've just made, it is helpful to be able to go back and view the history of our repository. One of the easiest ways to do this is to use the git log command. When no arguments are passed to it, git log will show you all of the commits in your repository, starting with your most recent changes and descending chronologically from there:

```
$ git log
commit ca476b6c41721cb74181085fd24a40e48ed991ab
Author: Chad Russell <chad@intuitivereason.com>
Date:   Tue Mar 31 12:25:36 2015 -0400

    Updated README

commit dc56de647ea8edb80037a2fc5e522eec32eca626
Author: Chad Russell <chad@intuitivereason.com>
Date:   Tue Mar 31 10:52:23 2015 -0400

    Initial commit. Added our README
```

There are a number of options and arguments you can pass to git log. You can limit the number of results by passing in a number as an argument; you can view the results for just a specific file; and you can even change the output format using the --pretty argument along with a number of different options. For example, if we wanted to see only the last commit to our README.md file and summarize the commit onto one line, we could use the following:

```
$ git log -1 --pretty=oneline -- README.md
ca476b6c41721cb74181085fd24a40e48ed991ab Updated README
```

To break down this command, we're telling it to limit it to -1 one result, to use the oneline pretty format, and -- README.md only for our README.md file.

■ **Note**   By far, the most frequent commands you'll use will be git add, git commit, git log, git pull, and git push. These commands add files, commit files to the repository, pull changes from a remote origin, or push local changes *to* a remote origin (such as a hosted repository—more on that later). However, there are a number of additional commands and sub-commands that Git makes available to perform various tasks. For a full list of commands you can use git --help, and use git --help a to show sub-commands available.

Ignoring Specific Files

There will often be a number of files and directories within your project that you do not want Git to track. Git provides an easy way of specifying this by way of a *Git Ignore* file, called .gitignore. You can save these anywhere within your project, but usually you'll start with one in your root project directory.

Once you create and save this file, you can edit it within your IDE or text editor and add the files and/or paths that you want to ignore. For now, I want to ignore the settings files that my IDE, PHPStorm, creates. PHPStorm creates a directory called .idea where it stores a number of files that are specific to my IDE's settings for this project. We definitely don't want that in our repository, as it's not related to the project specifically, and it could cause problems for other developers that clone this code and use PHPStorm. Our initial .gitignore file will now look like this:

```
# Our main project .gitignore file
.idea/*
```

For now, we have two lines; the first is a comment, which can be added anywhere in the file using the number sign #. The second is the line to tell Git to ignore the .idea folder and anything inside of it, using the asterisk to denote a wildcard match. We will then want to commit this file to our repository so that it's distributed to anyone else who may clone this repository and contribute back to it.

As your project grows and you have new files or directories that you don't want in your repository, simply continue to add to this file. Other items that are commonly ignored are configuration files that contain passwords or other system-specific information, temporary files such as caches, other media, or resources that are not directly needed by your project or even maintained within your development team.

Removing Files

At times you will need to remove files from your repository. There are a few different ways to approach removing files depending on the intentions of what you're doing.

If you want to completely remove a file from both the repository and your local working copy, then you can use the git rm command to perform this task. If you delete the file from your local copy using your operating system or within your IDE, then it will show up as a deleted file that needs to be committed.

Let's take a look. First, we'll create a simple text file to add to our repository, commit it, then delete it:

```
$ touch DELETEME
$ git add DELETEME
$ git commit -m "Adding a file that we plan on deleting"
[master 5464914] Adding a file that we plan on deleting
 1 file changed, 0 insertions(+), 0 deletions(-)
 create mode 100644 DELETEME
$ git rm DELETEME
```

```
rm 'DELETEME'
$ git status
On branch master
Changes to be committed:
  (use "git reset HEAD <file>..." to unstage)

        deleted:    DELETEME

$ git commit -m "Removed our temporary file"
[master 6e2722b] Removed our temporary file
 1 file changed, 0 insertions(+), 0 deletions(-)
 delete mode 100644 DELETEME

$ git status
On branch master
nothing to commit, working directory clean
```

Now, we'll delete it first on the local system and then remove it from Git, and then we will commit the change:

```
$ touch DELETEME
$ git add DELETEME
$ git commit -m "Adding another temporary file to delete"
[master b84ad4f] Adding another temporary file to delete
 1 file changed, 0 insertions(+), 0 deletions(-)
 create mode 100644 DELETEME
$ rm DELETEME
$ git status
On branch master
Changes not staged for commit:
  (use "git add/rm <file>..." to update what will be committed)
  (use "git checkout -- <file>..." to discard changes in working directory)

        deleted:    DELETEME

no changes added to commit (use "git add" and/or "git commit -a")
$ git rm DELETEME
rm 'DELETEME'
$ git status
On branch master
Changes to be committed:
  (use "git reset HEAD <file>..." to unstage)

        deleted:    DELETEME

$ git commit -m "Removing our second temporary file"
[master e980b99] Removing our second temporary file
 1 file changed, 0 insertions(+), 0 deletions(-)
 delete mode 100644 DELETEME
```

Lastly, you may find that you want to delete a file from Git so it's no longer tracked, but you want to keep the file locally. Perhaps you accidentally committed a configuration file that has now been added to your .gitignore file; you want to remove it from Git but keep it locally, for obvious reasons. For that you will use the --cache option along with the git rm command:

```
$ touch DELETEME
$ git add DELETEME
$ git commit -m "Adding a temporary file to delete one more time"
[master f819350] Adding a temporary file to delete one more time
 1 file changed, 0 insertions(+), 0 deletions(-)
 create mode 100644 DELETEME
$ git rm --cached DELETEME
rm 'DELETEME'
$ git status
On branch master
Changes to be committed:
  (use "git reset HEAD <file>..." to unstage)

        deleted:    DELETEME

Untracked files:
  (use "git add <file>..." to include in what will be committed)

        DELETEME

$ git commit -m "Removed temporary file just in the repository"
[master 26e0445] Removed temporary file just in the repository
 1 file changed, 0 insertions(+), 0 deletions(-)
 delete mode 100644 DELETEME
$ git status
On branch master
Untracked files:
  (use "git add <file>..." to include in what will be committed)

        DELETEME
```

Branching and Merging

Branching is a mechanism that allows you to separate various segments of changes to your code into sub-repositories of a sort. *Merging* is the method for bringing this code back together. For example, suppose you have your main-line repository that most development is performed under. Then you have some requirements to build a brand-new set of functionality into your application, but you'll still be making various unrelated changes and bug fixes to your existing code base. By creating a separate branch just for this new functionality, you can continue to make and track your changes to your main-line code and work on changes for the new functionality separately. Once you're ready to integrate this change into your main code, you will perform a merge, which will merge your changes into the main-line branch.

Note, however, that Git branches are not like a bridge to Subversion (git svn) branches, since svn branches are only used to capture the occasional large-scale development effort, while Git branches are more integrated into our everyday workflow.

To get started, let's create a branch for us to explore this functionality with:

```
$ git branch branch-example
$ git checkout branch-example
Switched to branch 'branch-example'
```

We created our new branch, called branch-example, with the first command. The second tells Git to switch to that branch so as to start working in and tracking changes there. Switching between branches is done with the git checkout command. Now, we'll create a test file for this new branch and commit it:

```
$ touch test.php
$ git add test.php
$ git commit -m 'Added a test file to our branch'
```

If we switch back to our initial branch (master) we'll see this file isn't there:

```
$ git checkout master
Switched to branch 'master'
$ ls
README.md
$ git log
commit e504d64a544d6a1c09df795c60d883344bb8cca8
Author: Chad Russell <chad@intuitivereason.com>
Date:   Thu Feb 26 10:23:18 2015 -0500

    Initial commit. Added our README
```

Merging

Once we're ready for our changes in the test branch to appear in the master branch, we'll need to perform a merge. When performing a merge, Git will compare changes in both branches and will attempt to automatically merge the changes together. In the event of a collision of changes, meaning that the same lines of code were changed in both branches, it will have you manually intervene to resolve the conflict. Once resolved, this will be tracked as another commit, and you can finish your merge.

Let's merge our branch-example changes into the master branch:

```
$ git merge branch-example
Updating e504d64..a6b7d2d
Fast-forward
 test.php | 0
 1 file changed, 0 insertions(+), 0 deletions(-)
 create mode 100644 test.php
```

Now that we've merged this in, in this case we don't need our branch-example any longer. We can simply delete it using the git branch command again:

```
$ git branch -d branch-example
```

Stashing Changes

There will be many times when working with your project that you might need to pull changes from a remote repository before you're ready to commit what you're working on, or you might need to switch to another branch to do some other work before you're ready to commit and don't want to lose your changes. This is where the git stash command comes in handy.

To stash your changes, you simply invoke the git stash command. You can view the stashes you've saved by passing in the list sub-command, and you can reapply the changes by using the apply sub-command. Let's see it in action:

```
$ git status
On branch master

Changes not staged for commit:
  (use "git add <file>..." to update what will be committed)
  (use "git checkout -- <file>..." to discard changes in working directory)

        modified:   test.php

$ git stash
Saved working directory and index state WIP on master: 08e9d29 adding a test
file
HEAD is now at 08e9d29 adding a test file
$ git status
On branch master

nothing to commit, working directory clean
```

You can see we had changes to test.php that weren't yet committed; after calling git stash we now have a clean working directory. See here:

```
$ git stash list
stash@{0}: WIP on master: 08e9d29 adding a test file
$ git stash apply
On branch master

Changes not staged for commit:
  (use "git add <file>..." to update what will be committed)
  (use "git checkout -- <file>..." to discard changes in working directory)

        modified:   test.php
```

```
no changes added to commit (use "git add" and/or "git commit -a")
$ git status
On branch master

Changes not staged for commit:
  (use "git add <file>..." to update what will be committed)
  (use "git checkout -- <file>..." to discard changes in working directory)

        modified:   test.php
```

We can see the stash we have saved using git stash list. We can reapply it and see it back in our working directory after calling git stash apply. By default, calling git stash apply will apply the most recent stash in the list. If you want to apply a specific stash, then you must supply the stash number that you see when calling git stash list. Using the preceding list output as an example, we would use the following:

```
$ git stash apply stash@{0}
```

Tagging

Tagging within Git allows you to tag any given commit with a label for future reference. For example, you can use it to tag specific releases of your code or other important landmarks along the way during development.

Git provides two different tag types. There's lightweight tags, which are just label pointing to a commit. Annotated tags are instead full checksummed objects that contain the name and email of the person tagging, and can include a message. It's highly recommended that you always use annotated tags unless you need to temporarily tag something, in which case a lightweight tag will do.

Lightweight Tags

Let's create a simple lightweight tag to demonstrate, then delete it and create an annotated tag.

Create initial lightweight tag:

```
$ git tag v0.0.1
```

Now show details of the tag:

```
$ git show v0.0.1
commit a6b7d2dcc5b4a5a407620e6273f9bf6848d18d3d
Author: Chad Russell <chad@intuitivereason.com>
Date:   Thu Feb 26 10:44:11 2015 -0500
```

```
    Added a test file to our branch

diff --git a/test.php b/test.php
new file mode 100644
index 0000000..e69de29
```

We can delete a tag using the -d option:

```
$ git tag -d v0.0.1
Deleted tag 'v0.0.1' (was a6b7d2d)
```

Annotated Tags

Now create the annotated version:

```
$ git tag -a v0.0.1 -m "Initial Release"

Show the details of the annotated tag:
$ git show v0.0.1
tag v0.0.1
Tagger: Chad Russell <chad@intuitivereason.com>
Date:   Sun Mar 15 18:54:46 2015 -0400

Initial Release

commit a6b7d2dcc5b4a5a407620e6273f9bf6848d18d3d
Author: Chad Russell <chad@intuitivereason.com>
Date:   Thu Feb 26 10:44:11 2015 -0500

    Added a test file to our branch

diff --git a/test.php b/test.php
new file mode 100644
index 0000000..e69de29
```

As you can see, on the annotated version we have the date, name, and email of the person who created the tag.

Undoing Changes

There will come times when you might accidentally commit something that you want to undo, or where you might want to reset your local working copy back to what it was from the last commit or a given commit within the repository history. Undoing changes in Git can be broken down in the following ways:

- Amend
- Un-stage
- File Reset
- Soft Reset
- Mixed Reset
- Hard reset

Amend

Undoing a previous commit by changing the commit message or adding additional files can be done using the --amend option with git. For example, suppose you have two files to commit, and you accidentally only commit one of them. You can append the other file you wanted to commit to the same file and even change the commit message using the --amend option, like this:

```
$ git add second.php
$ git commit -m "Updated commit message" --amend
```

Un-stage

This action would un-stage a file that has been staged but not yet committed. Un-staging a file makes use of the git reset command. For example, suppose you accidentally staged two files to commit but you only wanted to stage and commit one of them for now. You would use the git reset command along with the filename to un-stage it, like this:

```
$ git status
On branch master
Changes to be committed:
  (use "git reset HEAD <file>..." to unstage)

        new file:   first.php
        new file:   second.php

$ git reset HEAD second.php
$ git status
On branch master
```

```
Changes to be committed:
  (use "git reset HEAD <file>..." to unstage)

        new file:   first.php

Untracked files:
  (use "git add <file>..." to include in what will be committed)

        second.php
```

File Reset

A file reset would mean reverting your working changes to a file back to the most recent commit or to an earlier commit that you specify. To reset a file to the most recent commit, you will use git checkout:

```
$ git status
On branch master
Changes not staged for commit:
  (use "git add <file>..." to update what will be committed)
  (use "git checkout -- <file>..." to discard changes in working directory)

        modified:   first.php

$ git checkout -- first.php
$ git status
On branch master
nothing to commit, working directory clean
```

If you wanted to reset a file back to a specific commit, you would use git reset along with the commit hash and the filename, like this:

```
$ git reset a659a55 first.php
```

Soft Reset

A soft reset resets your repository index back to the most recent commit or a specified commit and leaves your working changes untouched and your staged files staged. It is invoked using the --soft option with git reset. You can either specify a commit hash to reset to or omit the commit hash, and it will reset to the most recent commit:

```
$ git reset -soft 26e0445
```

Mixed Reset

Much like a soft reset, a mixed reset resets your repository index back to the most recent commit or a specified commit, leaving your working changes untouched. However, it removes any files from staging. This is the default action of just using `git reset` or `git reset` along with a commit hash, such as:

```
$ git reset 26e0445
```

Hard Reset

Lastly, the hard reset is the most dangerous of all options, so use this only when absolutely necessary. It is a hard reset of your repository back to a given commit while discarding all working and staged changes. This action cannot be undone, so make sure you know that you want to do this before doing it:

```
$ git reset --hard e504337
HEAD is now at e504337 Added our first .gitignore file
```

Version Control in the Cloud: Bitbucket and GitHub

Having a remote-hosted repository is common practice when using Git other than for just your own personal projects. While there are many different ways of accomplishing this, there are two very popular services that allow you to have hosted repositories in the cloud. Enter Bitbucket (http://bitbucket.com) and GitHub (http://github.com).

Each of these services offers both free and paid plans. The largest difference in the free plan offered by both services is that Bitbucket allows an unlimited amount of private repositories, limited to five collaborators, and GitHub provides only public free repositories. Once you have an account with one of these services and create your repository, you will define this remote repository in your local Git configuration to allow you to push and pull changes to and from it.

Bitbucket

Let's get started with Bitbucket. When you first visit their site, you will create a new account. Once your account is created, you will log in and be provided with the option to set up a new repository. Before we proceed with creating our repository, there's a single step we can do that will make interacting with this repository a lot easier for us, which is adding an SSH key to use for authentication.

One of the most important advantages of Bitbucket is that it is JIRA integrated and also supports Mercurial.

SSH Key

You can add an SSH key to your Bitbucket account, which will allow you to interact with it from within Git on your local machine without having to type your Bitbucket password over and over again. To do this, navigate to the Manage Account section and then locate "SSH Keys." From here, you can add an SSH key from your local machine that will be used as authorization when working with any remote repository under your account. If you haven't ever set up an SSH key, it's easily done with Mac OS X and Linux, and by using Git Bash on Windows.

From within Mac OS X or Linux, open a terminal, or on Windows open a Git Bash prompt, then issue the following command and answer the few questions it presents you:

```
$ ssh-keygen -t rsa -C "chad@intuitivereason.com"
```

It is highly recommended that you accept the default values it provides, including the path to store the new key pair.

Once these steps are finished, you will have both a public and private key pair created. Locate the public key (using the path shown from the ssh-keygen process) and open it using your favorite text editor. You will then copy the contents of the public key to your Bitbucket account and save it. This will complete the key setup for your account.

Creating Your First Remote Repository

With the SSH in place in the Bitbucket account, you can now create your repository. To start, click the Create button located in the top navigation bar, which takes you to the Create form. Enter the information about your project and then click Create Repository. This will take you to the repository configuration page. This will provide you with a few options on what to do with this new repository. If you haven't yet created your local repository, as we did earlier, then you could use the "Create from scratch" option. However, in our case we want to push our current repository to this new remote Git repository. Following the instructions provided on this screen, let's link our repository and do the first push to it to copy our current code to it:

```
$ git remote add origin git@bitbucket.org:intuitivereason/pro-php-mysql.git
$ git push -u origin --all
Counting objects: 6, done.
Delta compression using up to 8 threads.
Compressing objects: 100% (3/3), done.
Writing objects: 100% (6/6), 524 bytes | 0 bytes/s, done.
Total 6 (delta 0), reused 0 (delta 0)
To git@bitbucket.org:intuitivereason/pro-php-mysql.git
 * [new branch]      master -> master
Branch master set up to track remote branch master from origin.
```

Now that we've successfully pushed it, we can click on the "Source" icon on Bitbucket to see our code visible there.

GitHub

Instead of using Bitbucket, you might want to use GitHub, and when comparing them we can say that they have very different billing structures and they also differ in history viewer and collaboration features.

The steps using Github are very similar. You first find and click the New Repository button, which will then present you with a Repository Create form similar to what we had with Bitbucket. From here, you'll fill out the form and create the repository. On the next screen, you'll be presented with instructions based on whether this is a new or existing repository, just as with Bitbucket. We can add this repository just like we did with Bitbucket:

```
$ git remote add origin git@github.com:intuitivereason/pro-php-mysql.git
$ git push -u origin --all
```

Pushing, Pulling, and Conflict Resolution

As we just did to initially push our code to our new remote repository, we'll use the `git push` command to continue to push code to it, as well as utilize the `git pull` command to pull code from the repository that may have been committed by others since our last pull.

For example, suppose you invite another developer to collaborate with you on a project. You pull the latest from the remote repository, then do some work. Developer 2 does the same, but commits and pushes his changes to the remote repository before you do. When you go to push, you'll receive a message back from Git telling you that your repository version is behind. You'll then use the `git pull` command to fetch any changes and attempt to automatically merge and rebase the changes with yours. Then you can push your changes to the repository. You'll both continue this pattern while both working with the repository.

In the event that both of you work on the sample file and have overlapping changes, Git won't be able to determine which version is the correct one to use. This is called a *conflict*. You must manually resolve conflicts, then commit the resolved changes and push back to the remote repository.

Git Tools

There are a number of tools that exist to make working with Git easier. Many IDEs offer integration with Git, and both Bitbucket and Github provide their own GUI tools that make working with Git much easier.

PHPStorm

If you're not familiar with PHPStorm, it is a popular, cross-platform (Linux, Mac OS X, and Windows) PHP IDE developed by JetBrains. It is the IDE that I use throughout the various examples; however, you do not have to have PHPStorm to do any of the exercises in this book.

You can download PHP Storm at:

```
https://www.jetbrains.com/phpstorm/download/
```

If you have a Git repository in your project root folder in PHPStorm, it will automatically detect it and provide menu entries to perform a number of different actions, as shown in Figure 1-1.

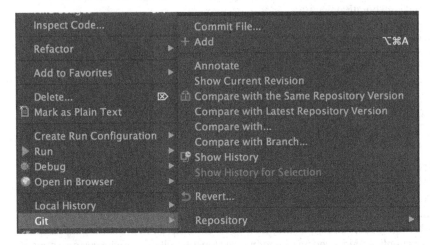

Figure 1-1. *PHPStorm Git menu entries*

Here we see there are a number of actions available to us when viewing these options while on our `test.php` file. From here we can commit or add the file, if it hasn't been added yet. We can also do a diff to compare our local file with the same version in the repository or with what the latest version might be on a remote repository. We can also compare it with another branch within our repository or see the history of all of the changes for this one file. Another function is the "Revert" function, which allows you to quickly revert any uncommitted changes in your file back to the state it was in for the last local commit.

Figure 1-2 shows the Repository sub-menu entry and the actions it provides within this sub-menu.

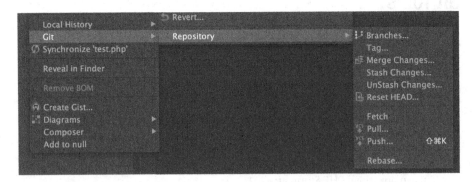

Figure 1-2. *Git Repository sub-menu entry in PHPStorm*

From this entry we can view branches, tag, merge, stash or un-stash our current changes, or fetch, pull, or push changes from and to a remote repository.

SourceTree

The SourceTree application is a free Git client for Windows and Mac users that is built by Atlassian, the same company that runs Bitbucket. It is a very powerful Git GUI client that makes working and interacting with Git repositories, both locally and remote, quite easy.

Installing SourceTree

SourceTree can be downloaded by visiting `http://www.sourcetreeapp.com`. Once downloaded, run the installer and follow the instructions to install it on your development machine. The first time you run SourceTree, it will prompt you to log in with an existing Bitbucket or GitHub account. You can either log in or skip this step. If you do choose to log in, you will be able to see your remote repositories within SourceTree's main bookmark/browser window. You can always choose to add one of these linked accounts later.

Adding a Repository

To add a Git repository to SourceTree, you will click on the New Repository button and choose whether you are cloning an existing remote repository, adding an existing local repository, or creating a new local or remote repository (Figure 1-3).

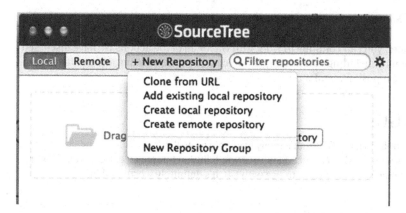

Figure 1-3. *Adding a new repository to SourceTree*

Add the new repository that you created earlier in this chapter by selecting "Add existing local repository." This will have you navigate to the directory where the repository was initialized, and then click the Add button. This repository will now be visible in the SourceTree bookmark/browser window. Simply double-click the name of the repository to bring up the full GUI (Figure 1-4).

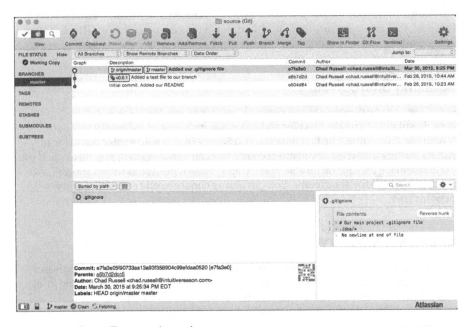

Figure 1-4. *SourceTree repository view*

From here, you can continue to work with Git for all of the actions we have discussed so far and others, including committing, branching, merging, pushing and pulling to and from a remote repository, and more.

GitHub GUI

GitHub has their own Git GUI that's freely available as well. It's very clean and intuitive to use, but lacks some of the advanced features you'll find in SourceTree. However, if you're looking for a nice, clean interface to use with Git, it's definitely worth looking at.

Installing the GitHub GUI

Like SourceTree, GitHub GUI is available for both Windows and Mac users. Mac users can download by visiting `https://mac.github.com`, and Windows users can download by visiting `https://windows.github.com`. Once downloaded and installed, GitHub will walk you through the setup process to finish the installation.

Adding a Repository

One interesting feature of the GitHub GUI is that it can find Git repositories on your system and provide them to you during setup, with the option of importing them in to start working with them in GitHub GUI. If you choose not to do that, you can also add or create a new repository later using the menu entry. Once your repository has been added to the GitHub GUI, you will be presented with the repository view, as shown in Figure 1-5.

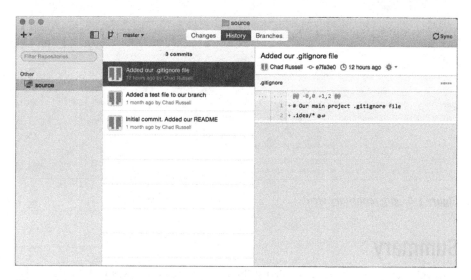

Figure 1-5. *GitHub GUI repository view*

gitg

gitg is an open source Git GUI that's made by the Gnome foundation and is for Linux users only.

Installing gitg

gitg is available for installation using both yum and apt-get. gitg doesn't quite provide the power and usability that is found with SourceTree, GitHub, or even within the PHPStorm IDE. It does, however, provide a nice interface for browsing or searching through a repository's history on Linux systems.

Adding a Repository

To add a repository using gitg, you click the "cog wheel" icon, which then reveals a sub-menu for opening a local repository or cloning a remote repository. Once added, you can click to open the repository view, as seen in Figure 1-6.

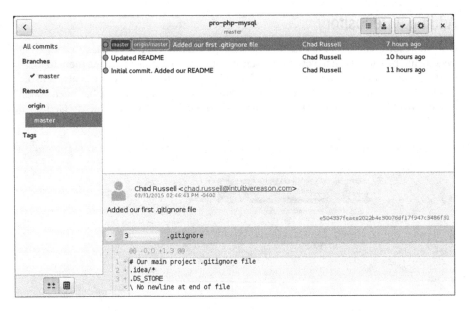

Figure 1-6. *gitg repository view*

Summary

In this chapter, we introduced the Git distributed version control system (DVCS). We covered the basics of using Git in day-to-day development, such as adding and committing changes, merging, and branching. We also covered working with remote repositories with the popular Github and Bitbucket services. We then discussed working with other developers and managing conflict resolution with committed files before reviewing some tools you can use to make working with Git even easier. Hopefully you're now moving on with a comfortable knowledge of Git and are able to start using it in your projects right away!

In the next chapter we will discuss virtualizing development environments.

CHAPTER 2

Virtualizing Development Environments

Creating virtualized development environments allows you to form encapsulated environments for specific projects that can have the same exact versions of operating systems, PHP, web servers, databases, libraries, settings, etc. as the real thing. These environments keep everything isolated from each other and can easily be destroyed and recreated as needed. This provides a number of benefits:

- Ability to run multiple projects on various PHP versions to match their production versions without trying to run them on your development machine.

- No chance of messing anything up with any configurations on your development machine when trying to install a library, change a setting, etc.

- Ability to take a snapshot of your environment that you can easily revert back to.

In this chapter, as we look into virtualizing your development environments, we will be focusing solely on using Vagrant, which is a tool for building complete, distributable development environments.

Traditionally, there are two approaches to setting up the development environment:

- Client and server processes run on the same machine.

- Client and the server run on different machines, which imitates the way the deployed application is executed by end users.

We'll look at the benefits of using virtualized environments, how to get and set up Vagrant, and how to provision your very first environment. By the end of the chapter you should be able to easily get up and running with your own virtual machine after running just one simple command: vagrant up.

C. Russell, *PHP Development Tool Essentials*, DOI 10.1007/978-1-4842-0683-6_2

Introduction to Vagrant

There's a good chance you have heard of or maybe even looked at using Vagrant before. As previously mentioned, Vagrant is a tool for building complete, reproducible, and distributable development environments.

■ **Note**   Vagrant is open source software distributed under MIT license.

It does this by following a consistent configuration pattern, allowing you to define sets of instructions to configure your virtual environment using Vagrant's specific language. These instructions are stored in a file called Vagrantfile, and since it is only text, it can easily be added to your project's source control repository, thus allowing the versioning of these environment configurations as well as allowing it to be easily distributed among other developers.

At the heart of it all, we can break a full Vagrant setup down into four pieces:

- Provider – This is the virtual platform that your Vagrant setup will run on. Since Vagrant doesn't provide any actual virtualization, it relies on providers to provide this functionality for you. By default, Vagrant supports VirtualBox. However, there are a number of other providers you can use, such as Docker, VMWare, Parallels, Hyper-V, and even cloud providers such as AWS and DigitalOcean.

- Boxes – Boxes are the virtual machine images used to build your Vagrant setup. They can be used by anyone and on any Vagrant provider. There are a growing number of public Vagrant boxes available for your use, some that are base OS installations and some with a preconfigured LAMP stack or other configurations and languages. In addition to the ones publicly available, you can also create your own Vagrant boxes that can be either shared publicly or used privately only by you and/or your team.

- Vagrantfile – Configuration file for Vagrant.

- Provisioners – Provisioners are used in Vagrant to allow you to automatically install software, alter configurations, and perform other operations when running the vagrant up process. There are a number of provisioners supported by Vagrant, but for the sake of this book we'll be looking at Bash, Puppet, and Ansible.

Installing Vagrant and VirtualBox

Before you can do anything with Vagrant, you must first have a virtual machine provider installed, such as the free and open source VirtualBox that we'll use throughout these examples. You of course also need Vagrant itself installed.

VirtualBox can be downloaded from its website, located at https://www.virtualbox.org. Simply download the appropriate installer package for your operating system and follow the instructions on the installer to install.

Like VirtualBox, Vagrant can be downloaded from its website at http://www.vagrantup.com. Download the appropriate installer package for your operating system and follow the instructions on the installer to install. Once installed, the vagrant command will be available to you in your terminal.

In this book we will use Vagrant for a Linux environment.

Vagrant Commands

All commands issued to Vagrant are done using the vagrant command that's now available to you in your terminal. Let's take a look at the list of command options we have:

```
$ vagrant -h
Usage: vagrant [options] <command> [<args>]

    -v, --version    Print the version and exit.
    -h, --help       Print this help.

Common commands:
    box              manages boxes: installation, removal, etc.
    connect          connect to a remotely shared Vagrant environment
    destroy          stops and deletes all traces of the vagrant machine
    global-status    outputs status Vagrant environments for this user
    halt             stops the vagrant machine
    help             shows the help for a subcommand
    hostmanager
    init             initializes a new Vagrant environment by creating a Vagrantfile
    login            log in to HashiCorp's Atlas
    package          packages a running Vagrant environment into a box
    plugin           manages plugins: install, uninstall, update, etc.
    provision        provisions the Vagrant machine
    push             deploys code in this environment to a configured destination
    rdp              connects to machine via RDP
    reload           restarts Vagrant machine, loads new Vagrantfile configuration
    resume           resume a suspended Vagrant machine
    share            share your Vagrant environment with anyone in the world
    ssh              connects to machine via SSH
    ssh-config       outputs OpenSSH valid configuration to connect to the machine
    status           outputs status of the Vagrant machine
    suspend          suspends the machine
    up               starts and provisions the Vagrant environment
    version          prints current and latest Vagrant version
```

```
For help on any individual commands, run `vagrant COMMAND -h`
```

```
Additional subcommands are available, but are either more advanced or are not
commonly used. To see all subcommands, run the command `vagrant list-commands`.
```

As you can see from the last bit of information outputted from this command, there
are additional subcommands that are available for us to use. For the sake of this chapter,
we'll be focusing on the most commonly used commands and subcommands.

Setting Up Our First Environment

With VirtualBox and Vagrant installed, getting up and running with your first Vagrant
environment is a relatively short and easy process. At a minimum, all you need is a basic
Vagrantfile and a selected Vagrant box to use.

For starters, we're going to set up a minimal install using a base Ubuntu 14.04 box.
Perusing the Hashicorp (the official company behind Vagrant) community box-repository
catalog, located at https://atlas.hashicorp.com/boxes/search, I see the box we want
to use is ubuntu/trusty64. Using two commands, we'll initialize our Vagrant setup,
download the box, install it, then boot our new virtual machine (VM).

The first thing you have to do is define Vagrant's home directory in the VAGRANT_HOME
environment variable. This can be easily done by executing the following command in bash:

```
$ export VAGRANT_HOME=/some/shared/directory
```

Let's create a new folder just for this Vagrant instance that we're setting up, then we'll
initialize the Vagrant setup:

```
$ mkdir VagrantExample1
$ cd VagrantExample1
$ vagrant init ubuntu/trusty64
```

You should see a message returned that tells you a Vagrantfile has been placed in
your directory and you're ready to run vagrant up. Before we do that, let's take a look at
the initial Vagrantfile that was generated:

```
# All Vagrant configuration is done below. The "2" in Vagrant.configure
  # configures the configuration version (we support older styles for
  # backward compatibility). Please don't change it unless you know what
  # you're doing.
Vagrant.configure(2) do |config|
  # The most common configuration options are documented and commented below.
  # For a complete reference, please see the online documentation at
  # https://docs.vagrantup.com.

  # Every Vagrant development environment requires a box. You can search for
  # boxes at https://atlas.hashicorp.com/search.
  config.vm.box = "ubuntu/trusty64"
```

```
# Disable automatic box update checking. If you disable this, then
# boxes will only be checked for updates when the user runs
# `vagrant box outdated`. This is not recommended.
# config.vm.box_check_update = false


# Create a forwarded port mapping, which allows access to a specific port
# within the machine from a port on the host machine. In the example below,
# accessing "localhost:8080" will access port 80 on the guest machine.
# config.vm.network "forwarded_port", guest: 80, host: 8080


# Create a private network, which allows host-only access to the machine
# using a specific IP.
# config.vm.network "private_network", ip: "192.168.33.10"


# Create a public network, which generally matches to bridged network.
# Bridged networks make the machine appear as another physical device on
# your network.
# config.vm.network "public_network"


# Share an additional folder to the guest VM. The first argument is
# the path on the host to the actual folder. The second argument is
# the path on the guest to mount the folder. And the optional third
# argument is a set of non-required options.
# config.vm.synced_folder "../data", "/vagrant_data"


# Provider-specific configuration so you can fine-tune various
# backing providers for Vagrant. These expose provider-specific options.
# Example for VirtualBox:
#
# config.vm.provider "virtualbox" do |vb|
#   # Display the VirtualBox GUI when booting the machine
#   vb.gui = true
#
#   # Customize the amount of memory on the VM:
#   vb.memory = "1024"
# end
#
# View the documentation for the provider you are using for more
# information on available options.


# Define a Vagrant Push strategy for pushing to Atlas. Other push strategies
# such as FTP and Heroku are also available. See the documentation at
# https://docs.vagrantup.com/v2/push/atlas.html for more information.
# config.push.define "atlas" do |push|
#   push.app = "YOUR_ATLAS_USERNAME/YOUR_APPLICATION_NAME"
# end
```

```
# Enable provisioning with a shell script. Additional provisioners such as
# Puppet, Chef, Ansible, Salt, and Docker are also available. Please see the
# documentation for more information about their specific syntax and use.
# config.vm.provision "shell", inline <<-SHELL
#   sudo apt-get install apache2
# SHELL
end
```

As you can see, most of the options here are commented out. The only configuration options line that isn't is:

```
config.vm.box = "ubuntu/trusty64"
```

This line tells Vagrant to use the box that we specified with our vagrant init command.

Initial VM setup

We're now ready to issue our next and final command, vagrant up. This will boot our VM for the first time and do any initial setup (provisioning) that we've told it to do. For now, this is just a basic system, so it will download the box we chose for the first time and import it, then just set up the initial SSH keys and make the machine available to us. See here:

```
$ vagrant up --provider virtualbox
```

You will see quite a bit of output from Vagrant as it downloads and brings up this initial box. The last few lines let you know it was a success and is ready for your use:

```
==> default: Machine booted and ready!
==> default: Checking for guest additions in VM...
==> default: Mounting shared folders...
    default: /vagrant => /Apress/VagrantExample1
```

We now have a new VM running Ubuntu 14.04. We can connect to this VM via ssh, just like on any other Linux machine. With Vagrant, we do this by issuing the vagrant ssh command:

```
$ vagrant ssh
Welcome to Ubuntu 14.04.1 LTS (GNU/Linux 3.13.0-45-generic x86_64)

...

vagrant@vagrant-ubuntu-trusty-64:~$
```

The Vagrant user is the default user set up with each box. This user has full sudo privileges without needing any additional passwords.

■ **Note**   Remember to run the command `vagrant -help` to get the entire list of commands you can use with Vagrant.

Shared Folders

By default, Vagrant will share your project's folder with the `/vagrant` directory inside of your VM. This allows you to easily edit files located directly in your project on your development machine and see those changes immediately reflected in the VM. A typical use for this would be to set up Apache on your Vagrant box and point the site root folder to somewhere within the `/vagrant` directory. Also, you can specify additional shared directories using the `config.vm.synced_folder` configuration parameter in the default Vagrantfile.

Networking

Vagrant provides multiple options for configuring your VM's networking setup. All network options are controlled using the `config.vm.network` method call. The most basic usage would be to use a forwarded port, mapping an internal port such as port 80 for regular HTTP traffic to a port on your host machine. For example, the following configuration line will make regular web traffic of your VM accessible at `http://localhost:8080`:

```
config.vm.network "forwarded_port", guest: 80, host: 8080
```

If you would prefer to specify a private IP address from which you can instead access the entire VM on your local network, you can use the `config.vm.network "private_network"` method call:

```
config.vm.network "private_network", ip: "192.168.56.102"
```

VM Settings

If you wish to change the amount of RAM or CPU that your VM is using, you can do so with the section of our Vagrantfile that starts with `config.vm.provider "virtualbox" do |vb|`. You will notice two entries there already that are commented out, one setting the Virtualbox GUI settings, the other setting the memory. If we want to change the memory as well as the default virtual CPU available to our image–to, say, 2048 MB memory and 2 CPUs–we can do so by adding the following under that section of our Vagrantfile:

```
config.vm.provider "virtualbox" do |vb|
    # Customize the amount of memory on the VM:
    vb.memory = "2048"

    # 2 virtual CPU's
    vb.cpus = 2
end
```

Before we apply this change, let's check to see what our VM is currently showing:

```
$ vagrant ssh
vagrant@vagrant-ubuntu-trusty-64:~free -m
             total      used      free    shared   buffers    cached
Mem:           489       331       158         0        12       207
-/+ buffers/cache:       112       377
Swap:            0         0         0


vagrant@vagrant-ubuntu-trusty-64:~$ cat /proc/cpuinfo
processor       : 0
vendor_id       : GenuineIntel
cpu family      : 6
model           : 58
model name      : Intel(R) Core(TM) i7-3740QM CPU @ 2.70GHz
stepping        : 9
microcode       : 0x19
cpu MHz         : 2700.450
cache size      : 6144 KB
physical id     : 0
siblings        : 1
core id         : 0
cpu cores       : 1
apicid          : 0
initial apicid  : 0
fpu             : yes
fpu_exception   : yes
cpuid level     : 5
wp              : yes
flags           : fpu vme de pse tsc msr pae mce cx8 apic sep mtrr pge mca
                  cmov pat pse36 clflush mmx fxsr sse sse2 syscall nx rdtscp
                  lm constant_tsc rep_good nopl pni monitor ssse3 lahf_lm
bogomips        : 5400.90
clflush size    : 64
cache_alignment : 64
address sizes   : 36 bits physical, 48 bits virtual
power management:
```

We can apply these changes to our Vagrantfile by running the vagrant reload command, which will be the same as doing a vagrant halt to shut down the VM and then a vagrant up to start it back up:

```
$ vagrant reload
```

Let's ssh in again and check our VM memory and CPU settings now:

```
$ vagrant ssh
vagrant@vagrant-ubuntu-trusty-64:~$ free -m
              total       used       free     shared    buffers     cached
Mem:           2001        208       1793          0         11         77
-/+ buffers/cache:         120       1881
Swap:             0          0          0

vagrant@vagrant-ubuntu-trusty-64:~$ cat /proc/cpuinfo
processor       : 0
vendor_id       : GenuineIntel
cpu family      : 6
model           : 58
model name      : Intel(R) Core(TM) i7-3740QM CPU @ 2.70GHz
stepping        : 9
microcode       : 0x19
cpu MHz         : 2702.438
cache size      : 6144 KB
physical id     : 0
siblings        : 2
core id         : 0
cpu cores       : 2
apicid          : 0
initial apicid  : 0
fpu             : yes
fpu_exception   : yes
cpuid level     : 5
wp              : yes
flags           : fpu vme de pse tsc msr pae mce cx8 apic sep mtrr pge mca
                  cmov pat pse36 clflush mmx fxsr sse sse2 ht syscall nx
                  rdtscp lm constant_tsc rep_good nopl pni ssse3 lahf_lm
bogomips        : 5404.87
clflush size    : 64
cache_alignment : 64
address sizes   : 36 bits physical, 48 bits virtual
power management:

Processor       : 1
vendor_id       : GenuineIntel
cpu family      : 6
model           : 58
model name      : Intel(R) Core(TM) i7-3740QM CPU @ 2.70GHz
stepping        : 9
microcode       : 0x19
cpu MHz         : 2702.438
cache size      : 6144 KB
physical id     : 0
siblings        : 2
```

```
core id          : 1
cpu cores        : 2
apicid           : 1
initial apicid   : 1
fpu              : yes
fpu_exception    : yes
cpuid level      : 5
wp               : yes
flags            : fpu vme de pse tsc msr pae mce cx8 apic sep mtrr pge mca
                   cmov pat pse36 clflush mmx fxsr sse sse2 ht syscall nx
                   rdtscp lm constant_tsc rep_good nopl pni ssse3 lahf_lm
bogomips         : 5404.87
clflush size     : 64
cache_alignment  : 64
address sizes    : 36 bits physical, 48 bits virtual
power management:
```

Removing VMs

Now, just as easily as we set up this VM, let's destroy it and all traces of it with another simple command, vagrant destroy:

```
$ vagrant destroy
    default: Are you sure you want to destroy the 'default' VM? [y/N] y
==> default: Forcing shutdown of VM...
==> default: Destroying VM and associated drives...
```

Just like that, our Vagrant VM is gone. However, our Vagrantfile is still intact, and the VM can be brought right back again by simply issuing another vagrant up.

Default Vagrant LAMP box

Our previous example is just a basic, bare Linux machine without Apache, MySQL, or PHP installed. This isn't very helpful if you're setting this box up for PHP development, unless you want to roll your own custom configurations.

Luckily, there are a number of community-provided Vagrant boxes that are already pre-configured with Apache, MySQL, and PHP, as well as some that already have popular PHP frameworks and platforms installed, such as Laravel, Drupal, and others.

Using the aforementioned Atlas community repository catalog or the Vagrantbox.es catalog (http://www.vagrantbox.es/), you can search and find a box that will work for you without any other configuration changes needed.

Advanced Configurations Using Ansible, Bash, and Puppet

As you can see from our initial example, it's extremely easy to get a VM up and running with Vagrant. However, just a basic VM isn't going to be of much use to us when setting it up as a full development environment that is supposed to mirror our production setup. If you don't find a Vagrant box that already has LAMP configured, then having to install and configure Apache, MySQL, and PHP manually each time you set up a new VM makes Vagrant a lot less useful.

It's also common that even if LAMP is already set up, there will be a number of configuration operations that need to be run after the initial setup, such as pointing Apache to a different public folder for your framework, or setting up a database for your application. This is where advanced configurations using one of the Vagrant-supported provisioners come in handy.

Vagrant supports a number of provisioners. For the sake of this chapter, we are going to look at Ansible, Bash, and Puppet. If you're only familiar with Bash, then it's the easiest to jump in and start using. However, there are many preconfigured packages available for Ansible (playbooks), Chef (recipes/cookbooks), and Puppet (modules) that will drastically cut down on the time it would take you to do these tasks even in Bash using basic commands.

Bash (Shell) Provisioner

Let's start with a simple example by installing Apache, MySQL, and PHP using a simple bash script. This entire Vagrant setup consists of two files–the Vagrantfile and our bash script. We're going to call this script provision.sh. This script will install the Ubuntu repo versions of Apache, MySQL, and PHP using apt-get.

We use the following line in our Vagrantfile to tell Vagrant to use Bash as a provisioner and then to use the provision.sh script:

```
config.vm.provision :shell, :path => "provision.sh"
```

The contents of our provision.sh script are as follows:

```
#!/bin/sh

set -e # Exit script immediately on first error.
set -x # Print commands and their arguments as they are executed.

export DEBIAN_FRONTEND=noninteractive

# Do an update first
sudo apt-get -y update

# Install Apache
sudo apt-get -y install apache2
```

33

```
# Install PHP
sudo apt-get -y install php5 php5-mysql php5-cli php5-common

# Install MySQL
echo mysql-server mysql-server/root_password password 123 | sudo debconf-
set-selections
echo mysql-server mysql-server/root_password_again password 123 | sudo
debconf-set-selections
sudo apt-get -y install mysql-server-5.6

# Restart Apache & MySQL to ensure they're running
sudo service apache2 restart
sudo service mysql restart
```

As you can see, with this script we're just running the same commands we would run if we were manually setting up our VM; however, we automate the process since Vagrant can run the Bash commands for us.

Puppet Provisioner

Puppet is a configuration management system that allows us to create very specialized Vagrant configurations. Puppet can be used to form many different types of Vagrant configurations via the inclusion of specific Puppet modules inside of your project. These modules can be obtained from the Puppet Forge site at https://forge.puppetlabs.com/. Each one of the modules you use will have anywhere from a few to many different configuration options so as to tailor the environment to your exact needs. You should reference the README for each one of these modules as you start customizing to find out what options are made available to you.

For this example, download the Apache, MySQL, and PHP manifests from Puppet Forge and organize them according to their recommended hierarchy as noted on the website. You should also download a few required dependencies from Puppet Forge as well. We'll use these to set up a VM with Apache, MySQL, and PHP just like with our Bash example.

■ **Note** A *manifest* is the instructions that tell Puppet what to do with all of the modules.

We'll place the Puppet manifest in the default location in which Vagrant will look for it, under manifests/default.pp. First, update the Vagrantfile to tell Vagrant that we're now using Puppet as a provisioner:

```
config.vm.provision "puppet" do |puppet|
    puppet.manifests_path = "manifests"
    puppet.manifest_file  = "default.pp"
    puppet.module_path = "modules"
end
```

Our directory structure is as shown in Figure 2-1.

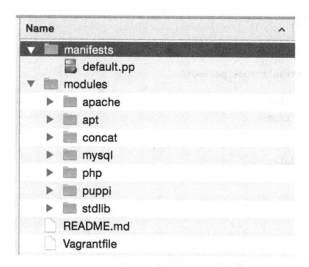

Figure 2-1. *Puppet Vagrant directory structure*

The default.pp file located under the main manifests directory is the file that tells Puppet what to install and configure for our VM. This is where you would define the various configuration options you need for your setup. For the sake of this example, I've kept the configurations simple and concise:

```
# Update apt-get
exec { 'apt-get update':
  command => 'apt-get update',
  path    => '/usr/bin/',
  timeout => 60,
  tries   => 3
}

class { 'apt':
  always_apt_update => true
}

# Install puppet in our VM
package {
  [
    'puppet',
  ]:
    ensure  => 'installed',
    require => Exec['apt-get update'],
}
```

```
# Install Apache, set webroot path
class { 'apache':
  docroot => '/var/www/html',
  mpm_module => 'prefork'
}

# Install MySQL, setting a default root password
class { '::mysql::server':
  root_password           => '123',
  remove_default_accounts => true
}

# Install PHP and two PHP modules
class { 'php':
  service => 'apache2'
}
php::module { 'cli': }
php::module { 'mysql': }

# Install and configure mod_php for our Apache install
include apache::mod::php
```

As you can see, there is a bit more going on here than we had in our Bash script; however, having the power and flexibility of being able to make configuration changes and specific installation setups just by adding in a few additional configuration parameters makes Puppet a great choice for complex setups.

Ansible Provisioner

Ansible is an automation tool that can be used for many types of autonomous tasks and is not limited to use with Vagrant. With Vagrant, we can use it along with a *playbook* to automate the setup and configuration of our Vagrant machines. An Ansible playbook is simply a YAML file that instructs Ansible on what actions to perform.

■ **Note**   You may want to consider running Ansible against the machine you are configuring because it can be quicker than using a combination of setup scripts.

Using Ansible is much more lightweight than using Puppet, as there is no need to download or include various modules to perform the tasks you need, and the guest VM doesn't need anything special installed. The only requirement is that the host machine running Vagrant have Ansible installed. Installation instructions for a variety of operating systems can be found in the Ansible documentation at http://docs.ansible.com/intro_installation.html#getting-ansible.

For this example, we'll configure a very simple Ansible playbook to set up Apache, MySQL, and PHP on our Vagrant machine, just like in our Bash and Puppet examples. First, we must instruct Vagrant to use Ansible as the provisioner and supply the name of our playbook file:

```
config.vm.provision "ansible" do |ansible|
    ansible.playbook = "playbook.yml"
end
```

Then we instruct Ansible to install Apache, MySQL, and PHP:

```
- hosts: all
  sudo: true
  tasks:
    - name: Update apt cache
      apt: update_cache=yes
    - name: Install Apache
      apt: name=apache2 state=present
    - name: Install MySQL
      apt: name=mysql-server state=present
    - name: Install PHP
      apt: name=php5 state=present
```

Even though this configuration seems very simple, don't let it fool you; Ansible is very powerful and can perform complex configurations. We can easily make configuration customizations—just as we can with Puppet—by making use of Ansible templates, variables, includes, and much more to organize and configure a more complex setup.

Advanced Configuration Conclusion

As you can see, utilizing provisioners to automate the tasks of completely building your environment makes setting up your development environments much easier than having to manually do it over and over again. Each provisioner has a different approach for how it accomplishes these tasks, giving you a range of choices and flexibility for you and your project or environment.

Configuration Tools

Now that we have a better understanding of some of the core configuration settings and provisioners available to Vagrant, let's take a look at two configuration tools aimed at making the setup of these environments even easier.

■ **Note** Both of these tools are under current development, so they're both constantly changing and progressing over time. It's been my experience with them that they're great for getting you up and running quickly, but they do have their periodic issues and weaknesses.

PuPHPet

This tool, pronounced "puffet," uses Puppet as the provisioning language and provides an easy-to-follow GUI for configuring your environment.

Accessing PuPHPet

You can access this tool by visiting https://puphpet.com, as seen in Figure 2-2.

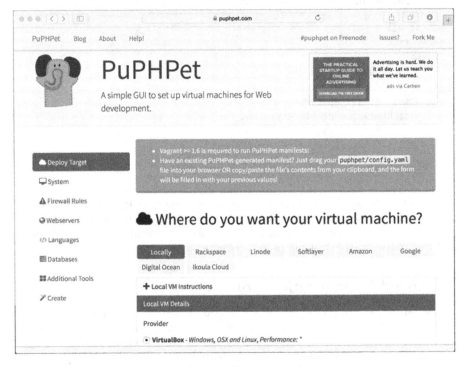

Figure 2-2. *PuPHPet web-based Puppet configuration tool*

PuPHPet is publicly hosted on GitHub, is open-source, and anyone can fork over and contribute to it. This tool works by generating a manifest YAML file along with the respective Puppet modules needed to build and configure your new VM environment. You can use the configurations it generates directly as is, or you can make modifications and tweaks as needed.

Setting Up and Using PuPHPet Configurations

Once you walk through each of the setup options on PuPHPet, you will download your custom configuration. This download consists of the Vagrantfile and a puphpet directory that contains all of the necessary Puppet manifests and modules needed for your environment.

Simply copy these two items to your project directory and you're ready to run vagrant up to set up and provision this environment.

■ **Tip**   One nice feature of the configuration setup generated by PuPHPet to note is the file structure under the `files` directory. This directory consists of four other directories, which allows you to create scripts that will execute once, every time, during startup, and so on. For example, you could utilize the `execute` once to perform post-setup cleanup, running custom commands needed to provision PHP application-specific dependencies (like `composer install`), as well as setting up databases data, etc.

Phansible

This is a newer tool that's become available, and it uses Ansible instead of Puppet as the provisioning language. It's similar to PuPHPet, but as of right now it does not have all of the bells and whistles that are available using PuPHPet. It also is publicly hosted on GitHub, is open source, and is available for anyone to contribute to (Figure 2-3).

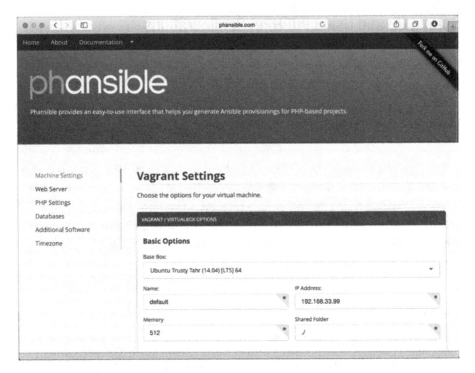

Figure 2-3. Phansible web-based Ansible configuration tool

Just as with PuPHPet, once you walk through each of the setup options on Phansible, you will download your custom configuration. This download also consists of the Vagrantfile and an ansible directory that has the playbook.yml file. It also holds several other items that can be used along with Ansible that we didn't utilize in our basic Ansible example earlier (such as the templates that were mentioned).

Phansible can be found at:

```
http://phansible.com/
```

Vagrant Plugins

As you begin using Vagrant more and more, you will periodically need additional functionality that isn't provided to you out of the box from Vagrant. Fortunately, Vagrant has a plugin system, and many times a plugin exists to do exactly what you need.

Vagrant plugins are very easily installed using the `vagrant plugin install plugin-name-here` subcommand. Here are a few helpful plugins that you may find useful as you begin to use Vagrant as your development environment choice:

- Vagrant Host Manager – This plugin manages the `hosts` file on the host machine, allowing you to easily specify a temporary `hosts` entry that maps to your VM's IP address. This allows you to easily set up access to your development environments using something similar to the production address. So if you have `www.someproduct.com` you could set up something like `dev.someproduct.com` or `www.someproduct.dev` and use the Vagrant Host Manager to automatically add this to your `hosts` file. It will add and remove this entry for you during the `vagrant up` and `halt` commands. This plugin is very useful when combined with specifying your own private network IP address for your VM. Additional information on this plugin can be found here: `https://github.com/smdahlen/vagrant-hostmanager`.

- Vagrant Share – This plugin, installed by default, allows you to share your environment with anyone, anywhere using a free account with HashiCorp.

- Vagrant Librarian Puppet – This plugin allows for Puppet modules to be installed using `Librarian-Puppet`.

- Vagrant Ansible Local – This plugin allows you to use Ansible as your provisioner, but instead allows Ansible to be run from within the guest VM rather than making the host machine dependent have Ansible installed.

- Providers – Although this isn't a specific plugin, there are many different plugins that allow Vagrant to be run on other providers, such as Parallels, KVM, AWS, DigitalOcean, and many more.

For a complete Vagrant plugin listing you can check this web page: `http://vagrant-lists.github.io/`

Summary

With the introduction of Vagrant, using virtual machines in your development process makes perfect sense. Hopefully, the topics covered here not only demonstrated this value you to you, but also gave you everything you need to be up and running with it on your next project or even on your existing project in no time flat. In the next chapter, we will discuss coding standards in order to define how to structure your code.

CHAPTER 3

■ ■ ■

Coding Standards

Coding standards are set definitions of how to structure your code in any given project. Coding standards apply to everything from naming conventions and spaces to variable names, opening and closing bracket placement, and so on. We use coding standards as a way to keep code uniform throughout an entire project, no matter the number of developers that may work on it. If you've ever had to work on a project that has no consistency in variable names, class or method names, and so on, then you've experienced what it is like to work through code that didn't adhere to coding standards. Imagine now how much easier the code would be to both follow and write if you knew the exact way that it should be structured throughout the entire project?

There are a number of PHP code standards that have waxed and waned in popularity and prevalence throughout the years. There are the PEAR Standards, which are very detailed; the Zend Framework Standard, which is promoted by Zend; and within the last five years or so, we've seen standards created by a board of developers called PHP-FIG.

Although this chapter is focused on PHP-FIG, there are no right or wrong answers on the standards you pick. The important takeaway from this chapter is that it's important to at least follow some standards! Even if you create your own, or decide to create your own variation that deviates a bit from an already popular existing one, just pick one and go with it.

We'll take a look at the PHP-FIG standards body and the standards they've developed and promote. We'll also look at the tools you can use to help enforce the proper use of given standards throughout your project's development.

A Look at PHP-FIG

PHP-FIG (php-fig.org) is the PHP Framework Interoperability Group, which is a small group of people that was originally formed at the phptek conference in 2009 to create a standards body for PHP frameworks. It has grown from five founding members to twenty, and has published several standards.

The PHP Standards Recommendations are:

- PSR-0 - Autoloader Standard
- PSR-1 - Basic Coding Standard
- PSR-2 - Coding Style Guide

- PSR-3 - Logger Interface

- PSR-4 - Autoloader Standard

For this chapter we'll look at PSR-1 and PSR-2, which stand for PHP Standard Recommendations 1 and 2. These standards are fairly straightforward, easy to follow, and could even be used as a solid foundation to create your own coding standards, if you wanted.

PSR-1 – Basic Coding Standard

The full spec of this standard can be found at http://www.php-fig.org/psr/psr-1/. This is the current standard as of the time of writing. This section is meant to give you a general overview of the standard and some basic examples of following it. The standard is broken down into the following structure:

- Files

- Namespace and Class Names

- Class Constants, Properties, and Methods

Files

The standards definitions for Files under PSR-1 are described in this section.

PHP Tags

PHP code must use <?php tags or the short echo tag in <?= format. No other tag is acceptable, even if you have short tags enabled in your PHP configuration.

Character Encoding

PHP code must use only UTF-8 without the byte-order mark (BOM). For the most part, this isn't one you have to worry about. Unless you're writing code in something other than a text editor meant for coding (such as SublimeText, TextWrangler, Notepad++, etc.) or an IDE, it's not something that should just automatically be included. The biggest reason this isn't allowed is because of the issues it can cause when including files with PHP that may have a BOM, or if you're trying to set headers, because it will be considered output before the headers are set.

Side Effects

This standard says that a PHP file should either declare new symbols (classes, functions, constants, etc.) or execute logic with side effects, but never both. They use the term *side effects* to denote logic executed that's not directly related to declaring a class, functions or methods, constants, etc. So, in other words, a file shouldn't both declare a function AND execute that function, as seen in the example that follows, thus enforcing better code separation.

```php
<?php

// Execution of code
myFunction();

// Declaration of function
function myFunction() {
  // Do something here
}
```

Namespace and Class Names

The standards definitions for namespaces and class names under PSR-1 are as follows:

- Namespaces and classes must follow an autoloading PSR, which is currently either PSR-0, the Autoloading Standard, or PSR-4, the Improved Autoloading Standard. By following these standards, a class is always in a file by itself (there are not multiple classes declared in a single file), and it includes at least a namespace of one level.

- Class names must be declared using StudlyCaps.

Here is an example of how a class file should look:

```php
<?php

namespace Apress\PhpDevTools;

class MyClass
{
  // methods here
}
```

Class Constants, Properties, and Methods

Under this standard, the term *class* refers to all classes, interfaces, and traits.

Constants

Class constants must be declared in all uppercase using underscores as separators.

Properties

The standards are fairly flexible when it comes to properties within your code. It's up to you to use $StudlyCaps, $camelCase, or $under_score property names; you can mix them if they are outside of the scope of each other. So, if your scope is vendor, package, class, or method level, just be consistent within that given scope. However, I would argue that it's really best to find one and stick to it throughout all of your code. It will make the uniformity and readability of your code much easier as you switch through classes and such.

Methods

Method names must be declared using `camelCase()`. Let's take a look at this standard in use:

```php
<?php

namespace Apress\PhpDevTools;

class MyClass
{
    const VERSION = '1.0';

    public $myProperty;

    public function myMethod()
    {
        $this->myProperty = true;
    }
}
```

This wraps up all there is to the PSR-1 Basic Coding Standard. As you can see, it's really straightforward, easy to follow, and easy to get a handle on just after your first read-through of it. Now, let's look at PSR-2, which is the Coding Style Guide.

PSR-2 – Coding Style Guide

This guide extends and expands on PSR-1 and covers standards for additional coding structures. It is a longer read than PSR-1. This guide was made by examining commonalities among the various PHP-FIG member projects. The full spec of this standard can be found at `http://www.php-fig.org/psr/psr-2/`. As with PSR-1, this is the current standard as of the time of writing. This section is meant to give you a general overview of the standard and some basic examples of following it. The standard is broken down into the following structure:

- General
- Namespace and Use Declarations
- Classes, Properties, and Methods
- Control Structures
- Closures

General

In addition to the following rules, in order to be compliant with PSR-2 the code must follow all of the rules outlined in PSR-1 as well.

Files

All PHP files must use the Unix linefeed line ending, must end with a single blank line, and must omit the close ?> tag if the file only contains PHP.

Lines

The standards for lines follow a number of rules. The first three rules deal with line lengths:

- There must not be a hard limit on the length of a line.

- There must be a soft limit of 120 characters.

- Lines should not be longer than 80 characters, and should be split into multiple lines if they go over 80 characters.

The last two rules seem to contradict themselves a bit, but I believe the reasoning behind them is that, generally, 80 characters has been the primary standard for lines of code. There are many, many arguments around why it's 80, but most agree it's the most readable length across devices and screen sizes. The soft limit of 120 is more of a visual reminder that you've passed 80 to 120, which is also easily readable on most IDEs and text editors viewed on various screen sizes, but deviates past the widely accepted 80. The no hard limit rule is there because there may be occasional scenarios where you need to fit what you require on a line and it surpasses both the 80- and 120-character limits.

The remaining line rules are:

- There must not be trailing whitespace at the end of non-blank lines.

- Blank lines may be added to improve readability and to indicate related blocks of code. This one can really help, so that all of your code does not run together.

- You can only have one statement per line.

Indentation

This rule states that you must use four spaces and never use tabs. I've always been a proponent of using spaces over tabs, and most any code editor or IDE can easily map spaces to your tab key, which just makes this rule even easier to follow.

Keywords and true, false, and null

This rule states that all keywords must be in lowercase as must the constants true, false, and null.

Namespace and Use Declarations

This standard states the following in regards to using namespaces and declarations of namespaces:

- There must be one blank line after the namespace is declared.

- Any use declarations must go after the namespace declaration.

- You must only have one use keyword per declaration. So even though you can easily define multiple declarations in PHP separated by a comma, you have to have one per line, with a use declaration for each one.

- You must have one blank line after the use block.

Classes, Properties, and Methods

In these rules, the term *class* refers to all classes, interfaces, and traits.

Classes

- The extends and implements keywords must be declared on the same line as the class name.

- The opening brace for the class must go on its own line, and the closing brace must appear on the next line after the body of your class.

- Lists of implements may be split across multiple lines, where each subsequent line is indented once. When doing this, the first item in the list must appear on the next line, and there must only be one interface per line.

Properties

- Visibility (public, private, or protected) must be declared on all properties in your classes.

- The var keyword must not be used to declare a property.

- There must not be more than one property declared per statement.

- Property names should not be prefixed with a single underscore to indicate protected or private visibility. This practice is enforced with the Pear coding standards, so there is a good chance you've seen code using this method.

Methods

- Visibility (public, private, or protected) must be declared on all methods in your classes, just like with properties.

- Method names should not be prefixed with a single underscore to indicate protected or private visibility. Just as with properties, there's a good chance you've seen code written this way; however, it is not PSR-2 compliant.

- Method names must not be declared with a space after the method name, and the opening brace must go on its own line and the closing brace on the next line following the body of the method. No space should be used after the opening or before the closing parenthesis.

Method Arguments

- In your method argument list, there must not be a space before each comma, but there must be one space *after* each comma.

- Method arguments with default values must go at the end of the argument list.

- You can split your method argument lists across multiple lines, where each subsequent line is indented once. When using this approach, the first item in the list must be on the next line, and there must be only one argument per line.

- If you use the split argument list, the closing parenthesis and the opening brace must be placed together on their own line with one space between them.

Abstract, Final, and Static

- When present, the abstract and final declarations must precede the visibility declaration.

- When present, the static declaration must come after the visibility declaration.

Method and Function Calls

When you make a method or function call, there must not be a space between the method or function name and the opening parenthesis. There must not be a space after the opening parenthesis or before the closing parenthesis. In the argument list, there must not be a space before each comma, but there must be one space *after* each comma.

The argument list may also be split across multiple lines, where each subsequent line is indented once. When doing this, the first item in the list must be on the next line, and there must be only one argument per line.

Control Structures

There are several general style rules for control structures. They are as follows:

- There must be one space after the control structure keyword.

- There must not be a space after the opening parenthesis or before the closing parenthesis.

- There must be one space between the closing parenthesis and the opening brace, and the closing brace must be on the next line after the body.

- The structure body must be indented once.

- The body of each structure must be enclosed by braces. This is definitely a very helpful rule, because it creates uniformity and increases readability with control structures and not having braces, even though it's allowed for single-line statements or when using the PHP alternate syntax, can sometimes lead to less readable code.

The next few rules are all basically identical for the following control structures. Let's look at simple examples of each of them.

if, elseif, else

This builds on the previous rule and states that a control structure should place else and elseif on the same line as the closing brace from the previous body. Also, you should always use elseif instead of else if so the keywords are all single words. For example, this is a fully compliant if structure:

```php
<?php

if ($a === true) {

} elseif ($b === true {

} else {

}
```

switch, case

The case statement must be indented once from the switch keyword, and the break keyword or other terminating keyword (return, exit, die, etc.) must be indented at the same level as the case body. There must be a comment such as // no break when fall-through is intentional in a non-empty case body. The following example is a compliant switch structure:

```php
<?php

switch ($a) {
    case 1:
        echo "Here we are.";
        break;
```

```
    case 2:
        echo "This is a fall through";
        // no break
    case 3:
        echo "Using a different terminating keyword";
        return 1;
    default:
        // our default case
        break;
}
```

while, do while

The while and do while structures place the braces and spaces similarly to those in the if and switch structures:

```php
<?php

while ($a < 10) {
    // do something
}

do {
    // something
} while ($a < 10);
```

for

The PSR-2 documentation shows that a for statement should be formatted as in the following example. One thing that is unclear based on what they have listed as well as based on their general rules for control structures is whether spaces are required between the $i = 0 and the $i < 10 in the example that follows. Removing the spaces and running it against PHP Code Sniffer with PSR-2 validation will result in it passing validation, so this is left up to you according to your preference. Both of the following examples are PSR-2 compliant:

```php
<?php

for ($i = 0; $i < 10; $i++) {
    // do something
}

for ($j=0; $j<10; $i++) {
    // do something
}
```

foreach

A PSR-2 compliant foreach statement should be structured as in the following example. Unlike in the for statement, the space is required if you are separating the key and value pairs using the => assignment:

```php
<?php

foreach ($array as $a) {
    // do something
}

foreach ($array as $key => $value) {
    // do something
}
```

try, catch (and finally)

Last in the control structure rules is the try catch block. A try catch block should look like the following example. The PSR-2 standard doesn't include anything about the finally block (PHP 5.5 and later), but if using it, you should follow the same structure as in the try block:

```php
<?php

try {
    // try something
} catch (ExceptionType $e) {
    // catch exception
} finally {
    // added a finally block
}
```

Closures

Closures, also known as anonymous functions, have a number of rules to follow for the PSR-2 standard. They are very similar to the rules that we have for functions, methods, and control structures. This is mostly due to closures being anonymous functions, so the similarities between them and functions and methods make them close to identical. The PSR-2 rules are as follows:

- Closures must be declared with a space after the function keyword and a space both before and after the use keyword.

- The opening brace must go on the same line, and the closing brace must go on the next line, following the body, just as with functions, methods, and control structures.

- There must not be a space after the opening parenthesis of the argument list or variable list, and there must not be a space before the closing parenthesis of the argument list or variable list. Again, this is the same as with functions and methods.

- There must not be a space before each comma in the argument list or variable list, and there must be one space after each comma in the argument list or variable list.

- Closure arguments with default values must go at the end of the argument list, just as with regular functions and methods.

Here are a few examples of closures that are PSR-2 compliant:

```php
<?php

// Basic closure
$example = function () {
    // function code body
};

// Closure with arguments
$example2 = function ($arg1, $arg2) {
    // function code body
};

// Closure inheriting variables
$example3 = function () use ($var1, $var2) {
    // function code body
};
```

Just as with functions and methods, argument lists and variable lists may be split across multiple lines. The same rules that apply to functions and methods apply to closures.

Lastly, if a closure is being used directly in a function or method call as an argument, it must still follow and use the same formatting rules. For example:

```php
<?php

$myClass->method(
    $arg1,
    function () {
        // function code body
    }
);
```

These rules conclude the PSR-2 Coding Style Guide. As you can see, they build on the basic rules set forth in PSR-1, and most of them build on rules from each other and share a number of commonalities.

Omissions from PSR-2

There are many elements that were intentionally omitted by the PSR-2 standard (although these items may eventually become part of the specification over time). These omissions include but are not limited to the following, according to the PSR-2 specification:

> Declaration of global variables and global constants
>
> Declaration of functions
>
> Operations and assignment
>
> Inter-line alignment
>
> Comments and documentation blocks
>
> Class name prefixes and suffixes
>
> Best practices

Checking Coding Standards with PHP Code Sniffer

Coding standards are a great thing to have, and online resources, such as the documentation provided by PHP-FIG on PSR-1 and PSR-2, help aid you in making the correct choices so that your code is compliant. However, it's still easy to forget a rule or mistype something to make it invalid, or maybe you're part of a team and it's impossible to do code reviews on everyone's code to make sure all of their commits are compliant. This is where it's good to have a code validator that everyone can easily run, or that could even be incorporated into an automated process, to ensure all code is compliant with PSR-1 and PSR-2, or even with another coding standard that you choose.

A tool such as this exists, and it's called the PHP Code Sniffer, also referred to as PHP_CodeSniffer by Squizlabs. PHP_CodeSniffer is a set of two PHP scripts. The first is phpcs, which, when run, will tokenize PHP files (as well as JavaScript and CSS) to detect violations of a defined coding standard. The second script is phpcbf, which can be used to automatically correct coding standard violations.

PHP_CodeSniffer can be installed a number of different ways. You can download the Phar files for each of the two commands, you can install using Pear, or you can install using Composer. Here are the steps for each of these installation methods.

1. Downloading and executing Phar files:

   ```
   $ curl -OL https://squizlabs.github.io/PHP_CodeSniffer/phpcs.phar
   ```

   ```
   $ curl -OL https://squizlabs.github.io/PHP_CodeSniffer/phpcbf.phar
   ```

2. If you have Pear installed you can install it using the PEAR installer. This is done by the following command:

   ```
   $ pear install PHP_CodeSniffer
   ```

3. Lastly, if you use and are familiar with Composer (using
   Composer is covered in Chapter 4) then you can install it
   system-wide with the following command:

```
$ composer global require "squizlabs/php_codesniffer=*"
```

Using PHP_CodeSniffer

Once you have installed PHP_CodeSniffer, you can use it either via command line or
directly in some IDEs, such as PHP Storm or NetBeans. Using it from the command line is
the quickest way to get started using it. You can use it to validate a single file or an entire
directory.

■ **Note** One PHP_CodeSniffer prerequisite is that the PEAR package manager is installed
on the machine.

Right now, you can find two files, named invalid.php and valid.php, in the
"Chapter3" branch of the accompanying code repository for this book. We're going to test
PHP_CodeSniffer against these files:

```
$ phpcs --standard=PSR1,PSR2 invalid.php

FILE: /Apress/source/invalid.php
--------------------------------------------------------------------
FOUND 10 ERRORS AFFECTING 5 LINES
--------------------------------------------------------------------
 3 | ERROR | [ ] Each class must be in a namespace of at least one
   |       |     level (a top-level vendor name)
 3 | ERROR | [x] Opening brace of a class must be on the line after
   |       |     the definition
 4 | ERROR | [ ] Class constants must be uppercase; expected VERSION
   |       |     but found version
 6 | ERROR | [ ] The var keyword must not be used to declare a
   |       |     property
 6 | ERROR | [ ] Visibility must be declared on property "$Property"
 8 | ERROR | [ ] Method name "ExampleClass::ExampleMethod" is not in
   |       |     camel caps format
 8 | ERROR | [ ] Expected "function abc(...)"; found "function abc
   |       |     (...)"
```

```
 8 | ERROR | [x] Expected 0 spaces before opening parenthesis; 1
   |       |     found
 8 | ERROR | [x] Opening brace should be on a new line
11 | ERROR | [x] Expected 1 newline at end of file; 0 found
----------------------------------------------------------------------
PHPCBF CAN FIX THE 4 MARKED SNIFF VIOLATIONS AUTOMATICALLY
----------------------------------------------------------------------
```

From this output we see there are ten different errors that were detected when validating against the PSR-1 and PSR-2 standards. You can pass in different standards to be used for validating, and even pass multiple standards separated by a comma, as in this example using PSR1 and PSR2. Also, out of the ten errors, four were marked as able to be fixed automatically using the PHP Code Beautifier and Fixer, otherwise known as the phpcbf tool. We can now run phpcbf against the file and try the validation again to see if it fixes it:

```
$ phpcbf --standard=PSR1,PSR2 invalid.php
Changing into directory /Apress/source
Processing invalid.php [PHP => 52 tokens in 11 lines]... DONE in 4ms (4
fixable violations)
        => Fixing file: 0/4 violations remaining [made 3 passes]... DONE in 7ms
Patched 1 file
```

As you can see, phpcbf is used just like phpcs in that you can pass in a list of standards to use to correct for, and then the file name. Now, to run the validator on the file again:

```
$ phpcs --standard=PSR1,PSR2 invalid.php
FILE: /Apress/source/invalid.php
----------------------------------------------------------------------
FOUND 5 ERRORS AFFECTING 4 LINES
----------------------------------------------------------------------
 3 | ERROR | Each class must be in a namespace of at least one level
   |       | (a top-level vendor name)
 5 | ERROR | Class constants must be uppercase; expected VERSION but
   |       | found version
 7 | ERROR | The var keyword must not be used to declare a property
 7 | ERROR | Visibility must be declared on property "$Property"
 9 | ERROR | Method name "ExampleClass::ExampleMethod" is not in
   |       | camel caps format
----------------------------------------------------------------------
```

Running the test after running phpcbf, we see it actually fixed one additional issue when it fixed another, so now there are only five errors found. Now, if we run it against our valid.php file, which is completely valid, we'll see what a valid result looks like:

```
$ phpcs --standard=PSR1,PSR2 valid.php
$
```

With a 100 percent valid file, there is no output from phpcs, indicating that it is valid. Now, if we wanted to run it against our entire directory, all we need to do is to point it at the source directory where our files are. However, doing this and seeing errors for every file in a large directory could be really hard to read through.

To help with this, PHP_CodeSniffer also has a summary report function that can summarize each file and the number of errors and warnings found in each. It is invoked by passing in the --report=summary argument. As with running it directly against a valid file, if there are no issues, it will not be listed on the summary:

```
$ phpcs --report=summary --standard=PSR1,PSR2 source
PHP CODE SNIFFER REPORT SUMMARY
----------------------------------------------------------------------------
FILE                                                      ERRORS   WARNINGS
----------------------------------------------------------------------------
.../Apress/source/invalid.php             5           0
----------------------------------------------------------------------------
A TOTAL OF 5 ERRORS AND 0 WARNINGS WERE FOUND IN 1 FILES
----------------------------------------------------------------------------
```

PHP_CodeSniffer Configuration

There are a number of different configuration options and methods for configuring PHP_CodeSniffer. Going through all of them is out of the scope of this chapter, so the online documentation listed earlier is the best resource for finding all available options. However, let's look at a few different options and how we can set them.

■ **Note** PHP_codeSniffer can also run in batch mode if needed.

Default configurations can be changed using the --config-set argument. For example, to change the default standard to check against to be PSR-1 and PSR-2 rather than the PEAR standard that phpcs uses by default, it could be set this way:

```
$ phpcs --config-set default_standard PSR1,PSR2
Config value "default_standard" added successfully
```

You can also specify default configuration options directly in a project using a phpcs.xml file. This will be used if you run phpcs in a directory without any other arguments. Here is an example:

```
<?xml version="1.0"?>
<ruleset name="Apress_PhpDevTools">
    <description>The default phpcs configuration for Chapter 3.</description>

    <file>invalid.php</file>
    <file>valid.php</file>
```

```
    <arg name="report" value="summary"/>

    <rule ref="PSR1"/>
    <rule ref="PSR2"/>
</ruleset>
```

Within this file, the files to check are specified, as well as the rules we want to use. Multiple rules are specified using multiple <rule /> tags.

PHP_CodeSniffer Custom Standard

In the event that you have your own standard, or have adopted most of PSR-1 and PSR-2 but decided to deviate from a rule here or there, you can create your own custom standard for phpcs to use. It is based off of the PSR-1 and PSR-2 standard and just overrides the parts that you wish to deviate from. This is done using a ruleset.xml file, which is then used with phpcs using the --standard argument, just as with any other coding standard.

At the very least, a ruleset.xml file has a name and a description and is formatted just as the phpcs.xml file we created is. However, just having the name and description does not provide phpcs with any instructions to override from an existing ruleset. For this example, say we want to change the standard to not restrict method names to camelCase. This would be done with a configuration like this:

```
<?xml version="1.0"?>
<ruleset name="Apress PhpDevTools CustomStandard">
    <description>A custom standard based on PSR-1 and PSR-2</description>

    <!-- Don't restrict method names to camelCase -->
    <rule ref="PSR1">
        <exclude name="PSR1.Methods.CamelCapsMethodName"/>
    </rule>

    <!-- Additionally, include the PSR-2 rulesets -->
    <rule ref="PSR2"/>

</ruleset>
```

With this ruleset, we see that all we needed to do was define a name for our rule, include the rulesets we wanted to base our standard off of, then specify the rule we wanted to exclude out of those rulesets. Now, if we run the validation against our invalid.php file we'll see the errors drop to four from five, as the method name violation is gone because our new standard doesn't restrict it to camelCase:

```
$ phpcs --standard=custom_ruleset.xml invalid.php

FILE: /Apress/source/invalid.php
------------------------------------------------------------------------
FOUND 4 ERRORS AFFECTING 3 LINES
------------------------------------------------------------------------
 3 | ERROR | Each class must be in a namespace of at least one level
   |       | (a top-level vendor name)
 5 | ERROR | Class constants must be uppercase; expected VERSION but
   |       | found version
 7 | ERROR | The var keyword must not be used to declare a property
 7 | ERROR | Visibility must be declared on property "$Property"
------------------------------------------------------------------------
```

PHP_CodeSniffer IDE Integration

As mentioned earlier, some IDEs such as PHPStorm and NetBeans have ways to integrate PHP_CodeSniffer directly within them. The exact process of configuring it for these IDEs can change as their respective vendors release new versions, so we won't cover this here. As of the time of this writing, the steps to set this up for PHPStorm are covered in the online documentation.

In my PHPStorm install, I have PHP_CodeSniffer configured and set to the PSR-1 and PSR-2 standards. With this configured, I get immediate feedback from PHPStorm if any of the code I'm writing deviates from these standards by way of a yellow squiggly line under the line of code that's in violation, as seen in Figure 3-1.

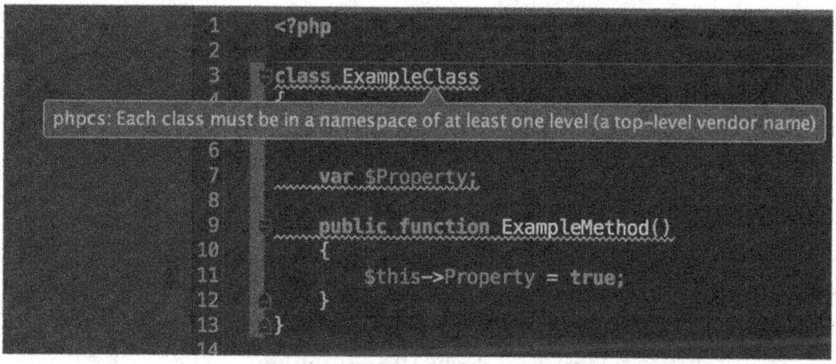

Figure 3-1. *Real-time PSR violation detection and hits in PHPStorm*

You can also run validation on the file and see the inspection rules directly within PHPStorm, as seen in Figure 3-2.

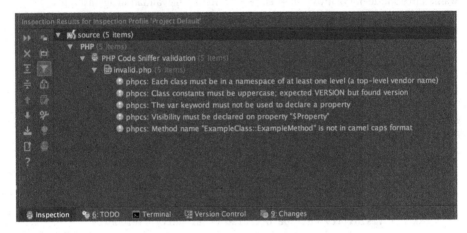

Figure 3-2. PHP_CodeSniffer validation results within PHPStorm

Code Documentation Using phpDocumentor

Not all coding standards provide rules regarding code comments. For example, PSR-1 and PSR-2 do not have set comment rules in place. However, it is just as important to establish a standard that everyone working on your project will follow when it comes to comments.

Arguably, one of the most popular formats for PHP is the DocBlock format used in conjunction with providing information about a class, method, function, or other structural element. When used in conjunction with the phpDocumentor project, you have the ability to automatically generate code documentation for your entire project and provide an easy reference for all developers to follow.

Another oft-used code documentation tool is PHPXref (phpxref.sourceforge.net). In general, PHPDocumentor and PHPXref have mainly two different targets:

- phpDocumentor is mainly used for generating real documentation from the source in a variety of different formats.

- PHPXref tool is mainly used to help the developer browse the code documentation of large PHP projects.

Installing phpDocumentor

phpDocumentor can be installed a few different ways. You can download the Phar file and execute it directly, you can install using Pear, or you can install using Composer. Here are the steps for each of these installation methods.

- First of all, you want to check the PEAR prerequisites:

```
http://pear.php.net/manual/en/installation.php
```

- Download and execute the Phar files:

```
$ curl -OL http://www.phpdoc.org/phpDocumentor.phar
```

- If you have Pear installed you can install it using the PEAR installer. This is done with the following commands:

```
$ pear channel-discover pear.phpdoc.org
$ pear install phpdoc/phpDocumentor
```

- Lastly, you can use Composer to install it system wide with the following command:

```
$ composer global require "phpdocumentor/phpdocumentor:2.*"
```

Using phpDocumentor

As previously mentioned, phpDocumentor should be used to document structural elements in your code. phpDocumentor recognizes the following structural elements:

- Functions
- Constants
- Classes
- Interfaces
- Traits
- Class constants
- Properties
- Methods

To create a DocBlock for any of these elements, you must always format them the exact same way–they will always precede the element, you will always have one block per element, and no other comments should fall between the DocBlock and the element start.

A DocBlocks' format is always enclosed in a comment type called DocComment. The DocComment starts with /** and ends with */. Each line in between should start with a single asterisk (*). The following is an example of a DocBlock for the example class we created earlier:

```
/**
 * Class ExampleClass
 *
 * This is an example of a class that is PSR-1 and PSR-2 compliant. Its only
 * function is to provide an example of how a class and its various properties
 * and methods should be formatted.
 *
```

```
 * @package Apress\PhpDevTools
 */
class ExampleClass
{
    const VERSION = '1.0';

    public $exampleProp;

    public function exampleMethod()
    {
        $this->$exampleProp = true;
    }
}
```

As we can see with this example, a DocBlock is broken into three different sections:

- Summary – The summary line should be a single line if at all possible and is just that–a quick summary of what the element is that we're documenting.

- Description – The description is more in-depth in describing information that would be helpful to know about our element. Background information or other textual references should be included here, if they are available and/or needed. The description area can also make use of the Markdown markup language to stylize text and provide lists and even code examples.

- Tags / Annotations – Lastly, the tags and annotations section provides a place to provide useful, uniform meta-information about our element. All tags and annotations start with an "at" sign (@), and each is on its own line. Popular tags include the parameters available on a method or function, the return type, or even the author of the element. In the preceding example, we use the package tag to document the package our class is part of.

■ **Note**   Each part of a DocBlock is optional; however, a description cannot exist without a summary line.

Let's expand on the preceding example and provide DocBlocks for each of the structural elements of our example class:

```
<?php

namespace Apress\PhpDevTools;

/**
 * Class ExampleClass
```

```
 *
 * This is an example of a class that is PSR-1 and PSR-2 compliant. Its only
 * function is to provide an example of how a class and its various properties
 * and methods should be formatted.
 *
 * @package Apress\PhpDevTools
 * @author Chad Russell <chad@intuitivereason.com>
 */
class ExampleClass
{
    /**
     * Class version constant
     */
    const VERSION = '1.0';

    /**
     * Class example property
     *
     * @var $exampleProp
     */
    public $exampleProp;

    /**
     * Class example method
     *
     * This method is used to show as an example how to format a method that is
     * PSR-1 & PSR-2 compliant.
     *
     * @param bool $value This is used to set our example property.
     */
    public function exampleMethod($value)
    {
        $this->$exampleProp = $value;
    }

    /**
     * Gets the version of our class
     *
     * @return string Version number
     */
    public function classVersion()
    {
        return self::VERSION;
    }
}
```

Now that we've expanded our example, you can see several unique tags being used as well as a sampling of how you can mix the three sections together as needed. For a full listing of the tags that are available for phpDocumentor to use, see the full phpDocumentor online documentation at `http://www.phpdoc.org/docs/latest/index.html`.

Running phpDocumentor

In addition to having nice, uniform code comments for your project when using phpDocumentor and the DocBlock format, you also now have the power and ability to effortlessly generate code documentation that will transform your comments into a documentation resource. Once you have phpDocumentor installed, it's simply a matter of running it to produce this documentation.

There are just two of three command line options needed to produce your first set of documentation. The options are:

- `-d` – This specifies the directory or directories of your project that you want to document.

- `-f` – This specifies the file or files in your project that you want to document.

- `-t` – This specifies the target location where your documentation will be generated and saved.

For this example, we'll run it against our one example class from before:

```
$ phpdoc -f valid.php -t doc
```

Here, we're telling phpDocumentor to run against the file `valid.php` and to save the documentation in a new folder called `doc`. If we look in the new `doc` folder, we will see many different folders and assets required for the new documentation. You can view it by opening the `index.html` file, which is generated in a web browser. We can see what the page for our Example Class looks like in Figure 3-3.

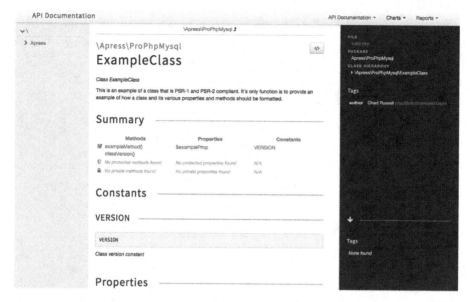

Figure 3-3. phpDocumentor-generated class documentation

Non-structural Comments

Lastly, since phpDocumentor only has provisions for structural comments, it is recommended that you establish guidelines for your coding standard that extend to non-structural comments. The Pear coding standard, for example, provides a general rule of thumb that is a great strategy to follow. Under their recommendations, you should always comment any section of code that you don't want to have to describe or whose functionality you might forget if you have to come back to it at a later date.

It's recommended that you use either the C-style comments (/* */) or C++ comments (//). It's discouraged to use the Perl/Shell-style comments (#), even though it is supported by PHP.

Summary

In this chapter, we discussed the benefits of using a coding standard for your projects. We took an in-depth look at the PHP-FIG PHP Standard Recommendations as well as some examples of code that follows these standards. We covered using the PHP_CodeSniffer tool as a validator of your code to ensure you and your team members are following your decided-upon standards. Lastly, we covered code commenting and documentation using the phpDocumentor project and the DocBlock format.

In the next chapter we will discuss Frameworks.

65

CHAPTER 4

■ ■ ■

Dependency Management

Dependency management is a system for easily managing (installing, using, updating, uninstalling) library dependencies in your project. The operative word in that statement is *easily*. For a long time, dependency management in PHP was virtually non-existent.

Of course, PEAR has existed since 1999, but it didn't fit the bill of providing easy dependency management within your application. It is used for globally installing packages server wide (think apt-get or yum), and anyone who has worked with PEAR's XML structure to create a package can attest to its lack of easiness. This is where Composer and its complement Packagist come into play.

Composer and Packagist

Composer is a command line tool that was created for easy dependency management in PHP applications. You define your application's dependencies in a single, simple JSON file format, and Composer will install and update those packages for you. It was inspired by npm and Bundler, which are the respective package managers for Node.js and Ruby, and borrows a number of features and concepts from both of them.

Installing Composer

There are essentially two different ways to install Composer. You can install it locally to your project, or globally as a system-wide executable. If you're just downloading it to check it out for the first time or don't have the access level to install it system wide, then a local install is fine. However, the best approach is to install it globally so that you have one Composer version that is installed and being used for all of your projects on the same server without your having to maintain various installs and versions.

Locally

To install Composer locally, simply run the following command in your project directory:

```
$ curl -sS https://getcomposer.org/installer | php
```

Once the installer runs, it will download the composer.phar binary to your project. You can then execute it by running php composer.phar.

© Chad Russell 2016
C. Russell, *PHP Development Tool Essentials*, DOI 10.1007/978-1-4842-0683-6_4

Globally

To install Composer as a system-wide executable, you will first download the `composer.phar` then move it to somewhere that is within your PATH on Unix-like systems (Linux/OS X, etc.):

```
$ curl -sS https://getcomposer.org/installer | php
$ sudo mv composer.phar /usr/local/bin/composer
```

You can now execute Composer by typing `composer` on the command line.

■ **Note**   If you are on a Windows system, then you can download the Windows Composer installer to install it globally on your system by visiting `getcomposer.org`.

Packagist

Packagist is the default Composer repository. It is a public aggregation of PHP packages installable via Composer. You can visit Packagist by visiting `packagist.org`, where you can easily search through the packages that are available. By referencing the version and package name, Composer knows from where to download the code that you are specifying in your project. As of the time of writing, it contained over 67,000 registered packages, nearly 314,000 versions, and boasted over one billion package installs since April 2012!

In addition to its being a searchable resource for developers looking for information on the packages they wish to install, package authors can easily submit their project to Packagist so that others can use Composer for the project as well.

Once your package has been successfully registered with Packagist, you can enable a service hook in your Bitbucket or GitHub account and have your package updated instantly when you push to your remote repository.

Using Composer

The only requirements to start using Composer in your project are to have Composer installed and to create your project's `composer.json` file. This file is where your project dependencies are listed, along with other possible metadata.

The composer.json File

In the most basic form, the only thing that is required is the use of the `require` key. For our example, we'll install the PHPUnit framework. We'll create the project's `composer.json` file like this:

```
{
  "require": {
    "phpunit/phpunit": "4.8.4"
  }
}
```

Now we'll install this framework with Composer, like this:

```
$ composer install
```

After running this command, we will see output from Composer as it downloads and installs all of the dependencies needed for PHPUnit, which will look something like this:

```
$ composer install
Loading composer repositories with package information
Installing dependencies (including require-dev)
  - Installing sebastian/version (1.0.6)
    Loading from cache

  - Installing sebastian/global-state (1.0.0)
    Loading from cache

  - Installing sebastian/recursion-context (1.0.1)
    Downloading: 100%
```

As Composer finishes its installation, you will see it generates a lock file and the autoload files needed to automatically load PHPUnit into your application. You will also have a new folder called vendor that includes all of the packages that Composer just installed.

Installing Additional Packages

Now, when you need to install additional packages into your application, you simply add the entry or entries for your new requirements to your composer.json file and run composer install again. Alternatively, you can make use of the composer require command, which will both add the entry to your composer.json file and install it in one command. For example, one of our application requirements might be to send emails, and we want to use the popular SwiftMailer library. To do this, we first look up SwiftMailer on packagist.com and find the package name, then we run the following command:

```
$ composer require swiftmailer/swiftmailer
Using version ^5.4 for swiftmailer/swiftmailer
./composer.json has been updated
Loading composer repositories with package information
Updating dependencies (including require-dev)
  - Installing swiftmailer/swiftmailer (v5.4.1)
    Downloading: 100%

Writing lock file
Generating autoload files ·
```

From the output, we can see it updated our composer.json file, installed the SwiftMailer library package, updated the lock file, and generated new autoload files. If you look at the composer.json file, you'll now see it updated to reflect SwiftMailer:

```
{
  "require": {
    "phpunit/phpunit": "4.8.4",
    "swiftmailer/swiftmailer": "^5.4"
  }
}
```

One thing you might notice with the new entry in the composer.json file is the version number for SwiftMailer—it includes the caret (^) operator. We'll dive deeper into Composer versions in a few sections, but for now this is the equivalent of telling future composer update commands that we always want the latest stable release that is >=5.4 < 6.0. If we wanted to be more specific with a version, like in the PHPUnit example, then we can optionally pass along a version to the composer require command, like so:

```
$ composer require swiftmailer/swiftmailer 5.4
```

Removing Packages

Composer makes adding new libraries to your application easy, and it makes it just as easy to remove packages that are no longer needed. There are two different ways this can be accomplished—either by manually removing the package declaration from your composer.json file and running composer update or by utilizing the composer remove command.

If we decide we want to remove the PHPUnit library we installed previously, we can do so with this single command:

```
$ composer remove phpunit/phpunit
Loading composer repositories with package information
Updating dependencies (including require-dev)
  - Removing phpunit/phpunit (4.8.4)
Writing lock file
Generating autoload files
```

require vs require-dev

Composer makes available two different methods of requiring a package. The first is by using the require declaration, as all of the previous examples have shown. The second is by using the require-dev declaration. You should always use require unless a certain package is only needed for the development of your application and not for running the application in production. A prime example for this would be a unit-testing library, such as PHPUnit. For example, let's now add PHPUnit back into our application, but this time specify that it's only needed for development using require-dev:

```
$ composer require phpunit/phpunit --dev
Using version ^4.8 for phpunit/phpunit
./composer.json has been updated
Loading composer repositories with package information
Updating dependencies (including require-dev)
  - Installing phpunit/phpunit (4.8.8)
    Downloading: 100%

phpunit/phpunit suggests installing phpunit/php-invoker (~1.1)
Writing lock file
Generating autoload files
```

Now if you look at the composer.json file, you will see phpunit has been added back, but this time under the require-dev declaration:

```
{
  "require": {
    "swiftmailer/swiftmailer": "^5.4"
  },
  "require-dev": {
    "phpunit/phpunit": "^4.8"
  }
}
```

The Composer Lock File

The Composer lock file is a list of the exact versions that Composer has installed into your project. This locks your project into those specific versions. It is important to add this lock file to your Git repository along with the composer.json file so that anyone working on your project will be using the same package versions. This is also important because if you're using any type of deployment scheme in your staging or production environments, you can utilize composer install to ensure those environments have installed the same exact versions of your packages that you have developed your application against. This also ensures that future updates to these libraries can be done within your application development, committed to your repository, and accurately distributed to these other environments. This also eliminates the need to store all of the various packages that Composer has installed in your source code repository.

■ **Note**   Because you track the dependency files and versions using the two Composer files now, there is no need to commit and maintain the vendor folder to your Git repository. You should add the vendor directory to your .gitignore file.

Autoloading

When using Composer, it will generate an autoload file vendor/autoload.php that is used to autoload all of your libraries and packages you have installed with Composer. Simply include this autoload file in your application (ensuring the correct path to the vendor/autoload.php file), and all of the installed packages will be available to you.

```
require __DIR__ . '/../vendor/autoload.php';
```

Now, if we wanted to use our SwiftMailer library we installed previously, we could do so simply by calling it:

```
// Create the SwiftMailer Transport
$transport = Swift_MailTransport::newInstance();

// Create a Mailer instance with our Transport
$mailer = Swift_Mailer::newInstance($transport);

// Create our message
$message = Swift_Message::newInstance('Learning Composer')
    ->setFrom(array('john@doemain.tld' => 'John Doe'))
    ->setTo(array('jane@doemain.tld' => 'Jane Doe'))
    ->setBody('Composer is wonderful!');

// Send our message!
$result = $mailer->send($message);
```

Additional Autoloading

In addition to autoloading all of the installed Composer library packages, you can utilize the Composer autoloader for your own application code as well. To do so, use the "autoload" field in your composer.json file.

For example, if you're storing your own application's code in a folder called src, you would add the following entry to your composer.json file:

```
{
  "autoload": {
    "psr-4": { "MyApplication\\": "src/" }
  },
  "require": {
    "swiftmailer/swiftmailer": "^5.4"
  }
}
```

This tells Composer to register a PSR-4 (The PHP-FIG Autoloading Standard) autoloader for the "MyApplication" namespace. Now, to get Composer to update vendor/autoload.php, you will need to run the dump-autoload command:

```
$ composer dump-autoload
Generating autoload files
```

In addition to PSR-4 autoloading, Composer also supports the PSR-0 autoloading, classmap generation, and file includes as valid autoloading methods. However, PSR-4 is the recommended method of autoloading with Composer for its ease of use.

Autoloader Optimization

Although not required for development environments, it is highly recommended that when generating the Composer autoloader for production use, you utilize the built-in autoloader optimizer. It is not uncommon to see performance boosts in your application up to 30 percent, especially if your application is spending a lot of time on the Composer autoload file.

There are two different ways to generate an optimized autoloader. The first is by using the dump-autoload command with the -o parameter:

```
$ composer dump-autoload -o
Generating optimized autoload files
```

For example, this command could be set up to run on staging and production environment deployments so that the standard autoloader is being used in development, but testing and production use are utilizing the optimized version.

In addition to generating the optimized autoloader via the dump-autoload command, you can also specify it in your composer.json file so that you are always generating the optimized version. This is done using the config directive:

```
{
  "autoload": {
    "psr-4": {
      "MyApplication\\": "src/"
    }
  },
  "require": {
    "swiftmailer/swiftmailer": "^5.4"
  },
  "require-dev": {
    "phpunit/phpunit": "^4.8"
  },
  "config": {
    "optimize-autoloader": true
  }
}
```

Package Versions

Composer provides a lot of flexibility when defining the version of a given package that you're installing in your application. You can essentially break down the definitions into three categories: basic constraints, next signification release, and stability.

Basic Constraints

Exact

Using basic constraints, you can tell Composer to install an exact version by specifying only the number, such as 1.2.4. This will ensure that your application is always using this exact version, regardless of the number of times composer update is run.

```
"require": {
    "vendor/packagea": "1.5.4"
  }
```

Range

Composer allows the use of comparison operators to specify a range of valid versions for your application. The valid operators are >, >=, <, <=, !=. In addition, multiple ranges can be specified using logical AND and OR logic. Separating a range by a space or comma is used to denote an AND and a double-pipe || is used to denote an OR. Here are a few valid examples:

```
"require": {
    "vendor/packagea": ">1.5",
    "vendor/packageb": ">2.0 <3.0",
    "vendor/packagec": ">2.0,<3.0",
    "vendor/packaged": ">1.0 <1.5 || >= 1.7"
}
```

Wildcard

In addition to specific versions and ranges, you can also specify a version number pattern by using a wildcard in the version declaration. For example, if we wanted any sub-version of the 4.2 branch of a package, it would be specified as:

```
"require": {
    "vendor/packagea": "4.2.*"
}
```

Range Hyphen

Another way of specifying ranges is with the use of a hyphen. When using the hyphen notation, partial version numbers on the right side of the hyphen are treated as wildcards. So consider the following example:

```
"require": {
    "vendor/packagea": "1.5 - 2.0",
    "vendor/packageb": "2.0 - 2.1.0"
  }
```

packagea in this example is the equivalent of >=1.5 <2.1. Since the version number on the right side is treated as a wildcard, Composer looks at it as 2.0.*.
packageb in this example is the equivalent of >=2.0 <=2.1.0.

Next Significant Release

There are two different operators you can use with Composer to define a version limit up to the next significant release of a given package.

Tilde

With the tilde operator ~ you can define a minimum version mark that you'd like to use for your application while protecting you from having to update to the next significant release of a package (the next x.0 release, for example). Consider the following example:

```
"require": {
    "vendor/packagea": "~2.5"
}
```

This declaration is the same as specifying >= 2.5 but <3.0. You can also define this at the sub-version level by defining your requirement as:

```
"require": {
    "vendor/packagea": "~2.5.2"
}
```

This declaration is the same as specifying >= 2.5.2 but < 2.6.0.

Caret

The caret operator ^ works very similarly to the tilde operator, with a slight difference. It is supposed to always allow non-breaking updates by sticking closer to semantic versioning. Consider the following example:

```
"require": {
    "vendor/packagea": "^2.5.2"
}
```

This declaration is the same as specifying >= 2.5.2 but <3.0. As you can see, this is slightly different than the tilde, which would have kept it from updating to 2.6.0. Lastly, regarding packages that are less than 1.0, the caret provides a bit of extra safety and will not allow such a large range of version updates:

```
"require": {
    "vendor/packagea": "~0.5"
}
```

This declaration is the same as specifying >= 0.5.0 but <0.6.0.

Stability

The Composer documentation can become quite confusing when trying to understand the stability of a package that Composer will install. Reading the "Versions" section of the Composer documentation would lead you to think that Composer might randomly pick a dev version of a package solely based on the constraint that you use when specifying the version.

Although this is technically true, this will only apply if you have specified the minimum stability to be dev in your composer.json file. By default, Composer will always select stable packages unless you specifically tell it otherwise using the -dev suffix under the require section, or if you have defined the minimum-stability configuration to dev.

Updating Packages

So far we've covered how to install and remove packages with Composer, as well as how to specify the version and stability of the packages your application relies on. The last major operation you will be doing with Composer will be to update your existing libraries. This is performed using the composer update command:

```
$ composer update
Loading composer repositories with package information
Updating dependencies (including require-dev)
Nothing to install or update
Generating autoload files
```

By default, when running composer update, a number of actions are performed. First, if you have made any manual changes to your composer.json file to add or remove a package, it will process those and will install or remove the given packages. Additionally, if any of your package versions are not locked to an exact version, it will look for any updates and install them according to your version specification. Lastly, it will regenerate the autoloading file and lock file and finish its operations.

There are a number of options you can pass to composer update. For example, by passing --dry-run you can see what Composer would do before actually doing it. You may choose to pass --no-dev, which will cause it to skip updating or installing any packages defined under the require-dev declaration. You can also define specific packages that you want it to update without updating all of the packages defined in your composer.json file. You do this by passing one or many packages to it, such as:

```
$ composer update swiftmailer/swiftmailer guzzlehttp/guzzle
```

Installing Packages Globally

Composer can be used to manage and install packages globally, similar to PEAR. This can be useful for installing certain utilities globally or even for maintaining updates to a global install of Composer itself.

As an example, if we wanted to update our global version of Composer, we would run the following command:

```
$ sudo composer self-update
```

If we wanted to install a utility such as PHPUnit, we would use a command like this one:

```
$ composer global require phpunit/phpunit
Changed current directory to /home/vagrant/.config/composer
You are running composer with xdebug enabled. This has a major impact on
runtime performance. See https://getcomposer.org/xdebug
Using version ^5.2 for phpunit/phpunit
./composer.json has been updated
Loading composer repositories with package information
Updating dependencies (including require-dev)
...
Writing lock file
Generating autoload files
```

Pay attention to the line that immediately follows when executing this command: Changed current directory to. This tells you it will install PHPUnit and its dependencies under /home/vagrant/.config/composer/vendor/. Our current user we're logged in as is "vagrant." which is why it chose this directory. You will need to add this directory to your global path for easy execution. Adjust the following command accordingly if you have a .bashrc or a .bash_profile file in your home directory. In my case, I have a .bashrc file, so that is what I'll use:

```
$ cd ~/
$ echo 'export PATH="$PATH:$HOME/.config/composer/vendor/bin"' >> ~/.bashrc
```

Now, reload to pick up the path changes, either by logging out and back in or by using the source command:

```
$ source .bashrc
```

You can now execute phpunit:

```
$ phpunit --version
PHPUnit 5.2.9 by Sebastian Bergmann and contributors.
```

PEAR & Pyrus

As mentioned in the introduction of this chapter, PEAR (the PHP Extension and Application Repository) was once the only method that tried to create a distributable system for providing libraries in your PHP application. However, PEAR has fallen short in many different areas, which paved the way for the creation of better tools for dependency management, like Composer.

PEAR did have some big successes, was and is still used by many different libraries and packages out there, and is still the system that PECL uses to install PHP extensions. The creation of PEAR2 and Pyrus over the last several years was intended to address a number of the shortcomings of PEAR, but they have not seen the traction and widespread community adoption and development that Composer has been enjoying. As a result, PEAR2 and Pyrus have been in alpha status for over four years as of the time of writing.

Is Anyone Still Using Pear?

The answer to this question–in my own opinion, in the opinions of other developers, and based on the current download statistics available on the Pear Download Statistics page–is both yes and no. The PHP7-compatible version of Pear has seen over 650,000 downloads since it was originally released in October of 2015, as of the time of writing. There are countless numbers of older PHP applications that still depend on various Pear packages, and therefore it is still in use with these. I do believe, based on our day-to-day development as well as the growing amount of libraries available on Packagist and the large number of open source platforms moving to use and support Composer (Zend Framework 2, Symfony Framework, Drupal 8, Magento 2, etc.), that the use of Pear as a library manager and for installing dependencies in applications is rapidly on a decline.

PECL

Despite the waning use of Pear overall, the PHP Extension Community Library, better known as PECL, is still quite active today. It is a public repository of PHP extensions and is often used to install libraries needed for development. PECL makes use of Pear for installing its libraries, which is evident when you look at the source of the pecl command:

```sh
#!/bin/sh

# first find which PHP binary to use
if test "x$PHP_PEAR_PHP_BIN" != "x"; then
  PHP="$PHP_PEAR_PHP_BIN"
else
  if test "/usr/bin/php" = '@'php_bin'@'; then
    PHP=php
  else
    PHP="/usr/bin/php"
  fi
fi

# then look for the right pear include dir
if test "x$PHP_PEAR_INSTALL_DIR" != "x"; then
  INCDIR=$PHP_PEAR_INSTALL_DIR
  INCARG="-d include_path=$PHP_PEAR_INSTALL_DIR"
else
  if test "/usr/share/php" = '@'php_dir'@'; then
    INCDIR=`dirname $0`
    INCARG=""
  else
    INCDIR="/usr/share/php"
    INCARG="-d include_path=/usr/share/php"
  fi
fi

exec $PHP -C -n -q $INCARG -d date.timezone=UTC -d output_buffering=1 -d
variables_order=EGPCS -d safe_mode=0 -d register_argc_argv="On" $INCDIR/
peclcmd.php "$@"
```

Now, let's look at the source of the peclcmd.php that is referenced in the last line of the pecl command:

```php
<?php
/**
 * PEAR, the PHP Extension and Application Repository
 *
 * Command line interface
 *
 * PHP versions 4 and 5
 *
 * @category   pear
 * @package    PEAR
 * @author     Stig Bakken <ssb@php.net>
 * @author     Tomas V.V.Cox <cox@idecnet.com>
 * @copyright  1997-2009 The Authors
 * @license    http://opensource.org/licenses/bsd-license.php New BSD
 *             License
 * @link       http://pear.php.net/package/PEAR
 */


/**
 * @nodep Gtk
 */
//the space is needed for Windows include paths with trailing backslash
// http://pear.php.net/bugs/bug.php?id=19482
if ('/usr/share/php ' != '@'.'include_path'.'@ ') {
    ini_set('include_path', trim('/usr/share/php '). PATH_SEPARATOR .
    get_include_path());
    $raw = false;
} else {
    // this is a raw, uninstalled pear, either a cvs checkout or php distro
    $raw = true;
}
define('PEAR_RUNTYPE', 'pecl');
require_once 'pearcmd.php';
/*
 * Local variables:
 * tab-width: 4
 * c-basic-offset: 4
 * indent-tabs-mode: nil
 * mode: php
 * End:
 */
// vim600:syn=php

?>
```

As we can see here, the `pecl` command is nothing more than a wrapper around the pear command. Every time you use `pecl` to install a new PHP extension or update an existing pecl extension, pear is being used. Because of this, it makes downloading, compiling, and installing needed PHP extensions very easy. For example, if we wanted to install the APC userland extension APCu, we would simply execute the following:

```
$ sudo pecl install apcu
downloading apcu-5.1.3.tgz ...
Starting to download apcu-5.1.3.tgz (108,422 bytes)
......................done: 108,422 bytes
39 source files, building
running: phpize
Configuring for:
PHP Api Version:         20151012
Zend Module Api No:      20151012
Zend Extension Api No:   320151012
...
install ok: channel://pecl.php.net/apcu-5.1.3
```

As simple as that, PECL and PEAR, along with `phpize`, have downloaded, compiled, and installed the APCu extension.

■ **Note**   If you are using the PHP version available from your operating system's repository (yum / apt-get) then you can check first to see if a PECL extension is already available to be installed directly from the repository. This will not require the use of PECL.

Should I Be Using PEAR or Pyrus?

Based purely on the current development state and activity of Pyrus and the many benefits and availabilities of packages with Composer and Packagist, I believe PEAR or Pyrus are no longer the best options to be used in new development today.

Because of the global installation nature of PEAR and the management it provides, it can still be a useful tool, and in some cases it is still the only tool for installing system-wide dependencies for certain utilities. Let's look at an example of installing the PHP CodeSniffer utility on a development machine using PEAR.

Installing a Global Utility Using PEAR

```
$ sudo pear install PHP_CodeSniffer
downloading PHP_CodeSniffer-2.5.1.tgz ...
Starting to download PHP_CodeSniffer-2.5.1.tgz (484,780 bytes)
...................done: 484,780 bytes
install ok: channel://pear.php.net/PHP_CodeSniffer-2.5.1
```

PHP CodeSniffer is now immediately available for your use. You can test if it is working like this:

```
$ phpcs --version
PHP_CodeSniffer version 2.5.1 (stable) by Squiz (http://www.squiz.net)
```

If you receive a warning when trying to run the previous command, such as PHP Warning: include_once(PHP/CodeSniffer/CLI.php): failed to open stream: No such file or directory, this means that your php.ini for the PHP CLI either does not exist or does not have the PEAR install path added to the php path. You can check this by following these steps, first checking the include path of pear installed on your system:

```
$ pear config-get php_dir
/usr/lib/php/pear
```

Now check which configuration file your PHP CLI is using:

```
$ php --ini
Configuration File (php.ini) Path: /etc/php/7.0/cli
Loaded Configuration File:        /etc/php/7.0/cli/php.ini
```

This will give more output than the preceding code, but you want to look for the Loaded Configuration File line.

Now, taking the path of the configuration file listed previously, check the PHP include path:

```
$ php -c /etc/php/7.0/cli/php.ini -r 'echo get_include_path()."\n";'
.:/usr/share/php:
```

So, as you can see, the include path does not include the pear include path. To solve this, we'll open php.ini and add it to the include_path directive like this:

```
include_path = ".:/usr/share/php:/usr/lib/php/pear"
```

If you try to execute the phpcs command again, it will now execute because it knows where to include the files from.

Summary

In this chapter, we introduced Composer and Packagist and how to use them together for your application dependency management. We covered, start to finish, everything you need in order to use Composer right away as well as the various daily interactions you will use Composer for as you manage the dependencies of your application. We also looked at PEAR and its role in today's PHP development.

My hope is that you walk away from reading this chapter with a very clear understanding of using Composer and the impact it can start making on your application development, and that you now have the resources and ability to use it right away.

CHAPTER 5

Frameworks

Chances are, even if you are very new to PHP, you've stumbled across at least a few PHP frameworks already. Symfony, Zend, Laravel, Yii, and CakePHP are just a few of the popular choices you have available to you.

When I first started developing with PHP back in 1999, there weren't any of these choices available. Back then, PHP applications were a jumble of logic, HTML, JavaScript, SQL queries, and more scattered across sometimes hundreds and thousands of files. Fast-forward a few years and a number of PHP frameworks started to take shape by 2005-2006, some of which are still around and thriving today (Symfony and Zend Framework, for example).

Admittedly, I originally resisted the notion of using one of these new frameworks. By this time I had started to evolve some type of defined structure for my sites and applications as I attempted to emulate MVC-esque structures and bring some type of separation and organization to the madness that I saw being developed all around me. I didn't want to throw that away and learn something quite so new to PHP. However, as these frameworks started maturing and community support started building, I realized that I didn't have a single good reason to continue the holdout. I dove headfirst into several of these popular frameworks and haven't regretted that decision once.

Why Use a Framework?

This is a question I am often asked by those who have yet to work with one. What is so special about a framework that I should use it rather than doing my own standalone PHP development? The benefits are many:

- A defined structure that becomes familiar across all of your sites and applications

- A community of folks who contribute to the betterment of the framework codebase and are available for questions–questions already asked and answered before (Stack Overflow, anyone?)

- A pre-developed set of functionality that you don't have to reinvent with each application

- Modules, libraries, and plugins available to you to instantly add additional functionality

C. Russell, *PHP Development Tool Essentials*, DOI 10.1007/978-1-4842-0683-6_5

- Better testability with likelihood of an existing integration with PHPUnit for unit testing

- Existing integration with ORMs

- Pre-established use of design patterns in your application. Often, using a framework means you're forced to conform at least somewhat to its paradigms, which can lead to better-structured and organized code

- Reusable and maintainable code purpose

For additional information about PHP and frameworks, please refer to phpframeworks.com.

■ **Note**   Frameworks are not a necessity with any PHP development. However, they are a highly valuable tool at your disposal to help you build a better application.

So, what do frameworks look like? Let's dive right in and look at a few widely popular and community-supported frameworks. With each of these framework examples, we'll look at:

- How easy it is to install

- Overall structure of the framework

- How to have a simple action and controller working

- How to make a simple database call and display the results

Zend Framework 2

We'll start by looking at Zend Framework 2. Zend Framework 2, colloquially known as ZF2, is the second generation of an enterprise-grade framework created by Zend Technologies. Zend Technologies is a company founded by Andi Gutmans and Zeev Suraski, who have contributed much to the development of PHP since its initial creation by Rasmus Lerdorf. ZF2 touts itself as being modular, secure, extensible, high performing, enterprise ready, and backed by a large and active community base. True to its modularity, ZF2 relies on Composer and is comprised of many components, all available via Packagist.

Installing ZF2

Installing and running Zend Framework 2 is extremely simple and fast.

■ **Note**   *ZF2* is not backward compatible with *ZF1* because of the new features in PHP 5.3+ implemented by the framework, and due to major rewrites of many components.

For this example, we'll install the ZF2 skeleton application, which is available on GitHub (https://github.com/zendframework/ZendSkeletonApplication) using Composer:

```
$ composer create-project -n -sdev zendframework/skeleton-application zf2
```

This command will install the ZF2 skeleton framework application in a folder called zf2. When it finishes, you should see a number of directories in the newly created zf2 folder (Figure 5-1).

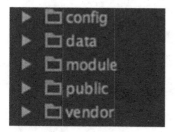

Figure 5-1. *Directories in the newly created zf2 folder following installation of the ZF2 skeleton framework application*

Each of these folders has a specific purpose and serves as the base structure of any ZF2 application. The functions of these folders are as follows:

- config – All global application configuration files are found in this directory. Things such as defining the modules in your application, database configurations, log configurations, and application-caching configurations are all contained here.

- data – This folder is a place to store application data. Things such as cache files, log files, and other such files would be stored here.

- module – The module folder is where all of your application logic is found. Here you will find all of the various modules that make up your application. We'll take a look at the folder structure of the module folder shortly.

- public – The public folder is the web-root of your application. In your webserver configuration, the document root will be set to this folder. Here is where all public-facing assets are stored, such as JavaScript, CSS, images, fonts, etc.

- vendor – This folder holds all of the third-party modules that you install in your application. This is the default place anything installed via Composer will go in your application.

The ZF2 skeleton application you just installed comes with a handy Vagrantfile that will let you quickly spin up a virtual machine that is running the skeleton application. Just as we covered running Vagrant in Chapter 2, to get it up and running you just need to run this:

```
$ vagrant up
```

Once it is installed, you should see the skeleton application in your browser (Figure 5-2).

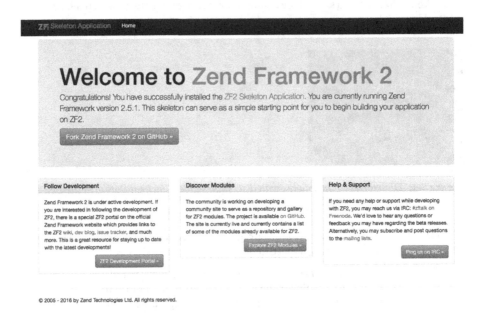

Figure 5-2. *The ZF2 skeleton framework displayed in a browser*

The purpose of this example is to explore how easy it is to define a controller and action and perform a simple database query within each framework. The ZF2 skeleton application already has a controller and action defined for us, which is what produces the welcome page you see in Figure 5-2. Let's take a look at the code that makes up this display as we deconstruct the `module` directory layout.

Module

Modules in ZF2 are where you compartmentalize groups of functionality in your application. ZF2 was built around the concept of a modular system. For example, if you have an application that has a user-facing side, an admin, and a set of batch processes, each could be separated into their own modules. For our example, if you expand the `module` directory, you will see the default Application module contained in the skeleton app (Figure 5-3).

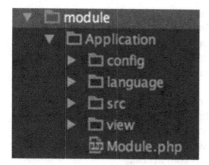

Figure 5-3. *The default Application module contained in the skeleton app*

This is the default structure of a ZF2 module; the folders each contain important pieces of your application, as follows:

- config – Here is where module-specific configurations are placed. Things such as routes, controllers, and view templates are defined.

- language – This is where translation files for your module would be found. The skeleton application uses the ZendI18n module and uses .po files to provide text translation.

- src – This is where the vast majority of your modules' code will live. This folder contains controllers, forms, services, and other application logic that makes up your module.

- view – The view folder contains your application views, the "V" in MVC. By default, ZF2 uses .phtml files, which is a pure PHP template approach for the presentation layer of your application.

- Module.php - This file contains the module class, which is the only thing ZF2 expects to have in order to instantiate your module. Here in this module, you can perform activities such as registering listeners, additional configurations, autoloaders, and more.

Controller

The controller is what ties the application actions to a view. The skeleton application contains the bare minimum required to make a controller and action work:

```
class IndexController extends AbstractActionController
{
    public function indexAction()
    {
        return new ViewModel();
    }
}
```

The naming convention of a controller class and file in ZF2 is `ControllerNameController` and `ControllerNameController.php` respectively. The `ControllerName` portion must start with a capital letter. Each action defined in the controller is a public method defined as `actionNameAction`. Actions must start with a lowercase letter. This follows PSR-1 standards for naming conventions of classes and methods.

Looking at the `indexAction` method in the preceding sample, the only code contained is returning the instantiation of `ViewModel()`. The `ViewModel` in ZF2 is responsible for setting and calling the appropriate view template for your application as well as for setting view variables and certain options that are available to you. By default, the `ViewModel()` will use the view named the same as your action.

Here is a simple example of controller and view models:

```
use Zend\View\Model\ViewModel;
```

Database

For our example, we're going to create a simple table that will contain the user's name and email address and then retrieve it and display it in our view. Although ZF2 supports powerful object relational mappers (ORMs), such as Doctrine, we're going to use the database extraction layer available to us in ZF2, called Zend\Db.

To get started, let's first create our simple database table and populate it with some simple data:

```
CREATE TABLE user (
    id int(11) NOT NULL auto_increment,
    name varchar(100) NOT NULL,
    email varchar(100) NOT NULL,
    PRIMARY KEY (id)
 );

INSERT INTO user VALUES
(null,'Bob Jones','bob.jones@example.tld'),
(null,'Sally Hendrix','sallyh@example.tld'),
(null,'Carl Davidson','cdavidson@example.tld');
```

Credentials Configuration

To be able to connect to our new database, we need to supply ZF2 with the configuration information for our database name, type, username, and password. This is done in the global config folder in the two files called global.php and local.php. Here we will also configure the ServiceManager that we'll use to connect everything together and then make it available to our application:

global.php
```
return array(
    'db' => [
        'driver' => 'Pdo',
        'dsn' => 'mysql:dbname=app;host=localhost',
        'driver_options' => [
            PDO::MYSQL_ATTR_INIT_COMMAND => 'SET NAMES \'UTF8\''
        ],
    ],
    'service_manager' => [
        'factories' => [
            'Zend\Db\Adapter\Adapter'
            => 'Zend\Db\Adapter\AdapterServiceFactory',
        ],
    ],
);
```

local.php
```
return array(
    'db' => [
        'username' => 'YOUR_DB_USERNAME_HERE',
        'password' => 'YOUR_DB_USERNAME_PASSWORD_HERE',
    ],
);
```

Model

Next, we'll create our model layer. The model layer for this example will contain a very simple representation of our table (entity) and another class to interact with the Zend\Db TableGateway that will perform our select query.

First, our entity, which is found under src/Application/Model/Entity/User.php:

```
namespace Application\Model\Entity;

class User
{
    public $id;
    public $name;
    public $email;
```

```
public function exchangeArray($data)
{
    $this->id = (!empty($data['id'])) ? $data['id'] : null;
    $this->name = (!empty($data['name'])) ? $data['name'] : null;
    $this->email = (!empty($data['email'])) ? $data['email'] : null;
}
}
```

This uses the exchangeArray, which you might recall is part of the PHP Standard Library (SPL), to map the data passed to it to the three methods that make up our table.

Next, the class that interacts with the Zend TableGateway is found under src/Application/Model/User.php:

```
namespace Application\Model;

use Zend\Db\TableGateway\TableGateway;

class User
{
    protected $tableGateway;

    public function __construct(TableGateway $tableGateway)
    {
        $this->tableGateway = $tableGateway;
    }

    public function fetchAll()
    {
        $results = $this->tableGateway->select();
        return $results;
    }
}
```

Service Manager

We use the ZF2 Service Manager to allow our new entity to be callable in our controller as a service. We do this by adding code to Module.php:

```
public function getServiceConfig()
    {
        return array(
            'factories' => array(
                'Application\Model\User' => function($sm) {
                    $tableGateway = $sm->get('UserTableGateway');
                    $table = new User($tableGateway);
                    return $table;
                },
```

```
            'UserTableGateway' => function ($sm) {
                $dbAdapter = $sm->get('Zend\Db\Adapter\Adapter');
                $resultSetPrototype = new ResultSet();
                $resultSetPrototype->setArrayObjectPrototype(new
                UserEntity());
                return new TableGateway('user', $dbAdapter, null,
                $resultSetPrototype);
            },
        ),
    );
}
```

View

The view name and folder structure in ZF2 generally follow the module namespace name, controller name, and action.

■ **Note**   The components of the view layer might be variables, containers, view models, renderers, etc.

Here is example code we're using from the skeleton app:

```
view (folder containing views)
- application (Namespace name)
  - index (controller name)
    - index.phtml (Action name)
```

View templates in ZF2 take a pure-PHP approach rather than a separate template language and use the .phtml extension by default. If you look at the index.phtml file available from the sample application, you will notice a mix of HTML and simple PHP.

Query & Display

The final steps will be to load our new users table as a service, query the whole table, and display the results. We'll do this by first instantiating the ServiceLocator, which is used to find and load services in our application. Then we'll have it specifically load our User class and return the instantiated object. See here:

```
<?php

namespace Application\Controller;

use Zend\Mvc\Controller\AbstractActionController;
use Zend\View\Model\ViewModel;
```

```php
class IndexController extends AbstractActionController
{
    protected $user;

    public function indexAction()
    {
        if (!$this->user) {
            $sm = $this->getServiceLocator();
            $this->user = $sm->get('Application\Model\User');
        }

        $users = $this->user->fetchAll();

        return new ViewModel([
            'users' => $users,
        ]);
    }
}
```

In this code, we got an instance of the ZF2 service locator and used the get method to retrieve our User model. Next, we queried the table and passed the results to our template using the ZF2 ViewModel object.

In our view, we'll add a new div and table and iterate over the results we are passing in using the ViewModel in our action:

```html
<div class="row">
    <div class="col-md-12">
        <div class="panel panel-default">
            <div class="panel-heading">
                <h3 class="panel-title">Users</h3>
            </div>
            <div class="panel-body">
                <table class="table table-striped">
                    <thead>
                    <tr>
                        <th>Name</th>
                        <th>Email</th>
                    </tr>
                    </thead>
                    <tbody
                    <?php foreach ($users as $album): ?>
                        <tr>
                            <td><?php echo $this->escapeHtml($album->name); ?>
                            </td>
```

```
                <td><?php echo $this->escapeHtml($album->email); ?>
                </td>
            </tr>
        <?php endforeach; ?>
        </tbody>
    </table>
        </div>
    </div>
    </div>
</div>
```

Now when we load our page again, we will see the results from the table we just queried displayed through our view template (Figure 5-4).

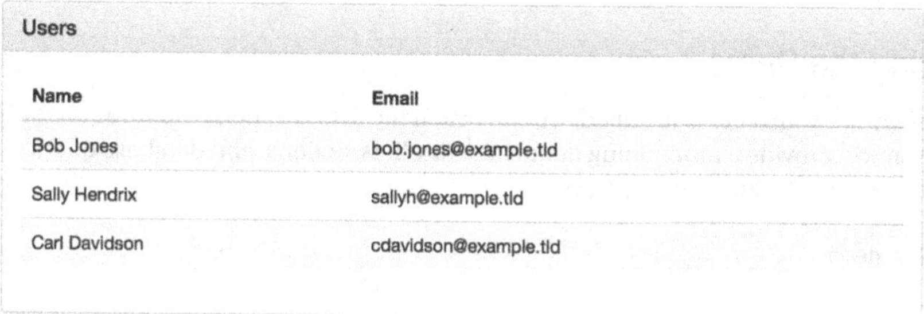

Users	
Name	**Email**
Bob Jones	bob.jones@example.tld
Sally Hendrix	sallyh@example.tld
Carl Davidson	cdavidson@example.tld

Figure 5-4.

Symfony 2

The next framework that we're going to look at is Symfony, specifically Symfony 2 (SF2). Symfony has been around about as long as Zend Framework and is another solid, reliable, enterprise-ready framework backed by a huge, vibrant community. Symfony, which is backed by SensioLabs, was started by Fabien Potencier back in late 2004 as a way to create websites faster for Sensio. Shortly after creating it, he decided to open-source it, and 11 years later, here we are with a community of thousands backing a great framework.

■ **Note** As of the time of writing, Symfony 3 has just been released. This tutorial focuses on Symfony 2 and the currently available Symfony Demo application.

Installing SF2

Although there are a few ways of installing Symfony 2 (SF2), the current best practice is to use the Symfony installer. To use the installer, simply run the proper commands for your operating system.

Linux and OS X

```
$ sudo curl -LsS https://symfony.com/installer -o /usr/local/bin/symfony
$ sudo chmod a+x /usr/local/bin/symphony
```

This will create a global symfony command that can be executed anywhere within your system.

Windows

Change to your project's directory and execute the following command:

```
c:\> php -r "readfile('https://symfony.com/installer');" > symphony
```

Installing the Demo

Once the Symfony installer is installed, we can install the Symfony demo application. This application will provide a functioning demo of controllers, actions, and database queries in SF2. To install this demo, simply type:

```
$ symfony demo
```

■ **Tip** The sample code provided with this book contains a Vagrantfile similar to what our ZF2 project provided to be used with the Symfony demo.

Application Directory Structure

Once the installer succeeds, you should see a number of directories in the newly created symphony_demo folder (Figure 5-5).

Figure 5-5. *Directories in the newly created symphony_demo folder*

Just as with ZF2, each of these folders has a specific purpose; they serve as the base structure of any SF2 application. The functions of these folders are as follows:

- app – This is a core folder to Symfony, in that it contains all configs, logs, cache file, the AppKernel, and autoloader and can contain other key data like views and translation files.

- bin – This folder is a place to store application data. Things such as cache files, log files, and other such files would be stored here.

- src – The module folder is where all of your application logic is found. Symfony application logic is compartmentalized into "bundles." Here you will have all of the various bundles that make up your application. This is very similar to the module folder for ZF2 we looked at. We'll take a look at the folder structure of a bundle shortly.

- vendor – This folder holds all of the third-party modules that you install in your application. This is the default place anything installed via Composer will go in your application.

- web – The web folder is the web-root of your application, just as the public folder is for ZF2. This is what your webserver configuration will set as the document root. Here is where all public-facing assets are stored, such as JavaScript, CSS, images, fonts, etc.

Once you have the demo installed and running, you should see the demo application in your browser (Figure 5-6).

Welcome to the **Symfony Demo** application

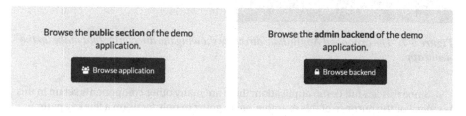

Figure 5-6. *The demo application running in a browser*

The SF2 demo application already has working controllers, actions, and database queries defined for us, which is what produces the sample application you see if you click the Browse Application button on the welcome page. Let's take a look at the code that makes up this functionality as we deconstruct the bundle and app directory layout.

Bundles

Just as with modules in ZF2, bundles in SF2 are where you compartmentalize groups of functionality in your application.

Using our demo application as an example, the primary app that you see is enclosed in the AppBundle bundle. The functionality that lets you view the source code on each demo application page is enclosed in a separate bundle, CodeExplorerBundle. For our example, if you expand the AppBundle directory, you will see the many directories that make up the demo app (Figure 5-7).

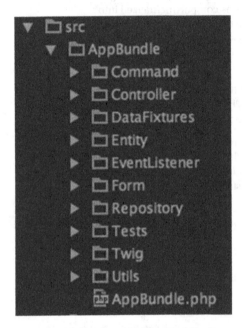

Figure 5-7. *The expanded AppBundle directory showing the directories that make up the demo app*

Since this is a full demo application, there are many other components set up in this bundle. For the purpose of this example, we're going to only focus on a few key parts, as follows:

- Controller – This is where all of the controllers contained within a bundle live.

- Entity – This serves mostly as the "M" in MVC (model) in that it contains all of the database entities that map the database to code.

- AppBundle.php – Similar to the ZF2 module.php, this file contains the AppBundle class and is what transforms the code contained in a bundle into functioning Symfony code.

One thing you may notice is the absence of our view templates within this bundle. Although it is possible to have your application views within your bundle–and in the past this was the normal place to keep them–according to defined Symfony best practices, it's best to contain them in the app folder in the app/Resources/views directory.

Controller

As we explored with ZF2, the controller is what ties the application actions to a view. The demo application contains a few controllers, but we're focusing on just the BlogController and indexAction for this example:

```
public function indexAction($page)
{
    $query = $this->getDoctrine()->getRepository('AppBundle:Post')->
    queryLatest();

    $paginator = $this->get('knp_paginator');
    $posts = $paginator->paginate($query, $page, Post::NUM_ITEMS);
    $posts->setUsedRoute('blog_index_paginated');

    return $this->render('blog/index.html.twig', array('posts' => $posts));
}
```

Just as with ZF2, SF2 controller-naming conventions follow StudlyCaps for controller file names and class names, and each action is defined in camelCase, again following PSR-1 standards.

SF2 uses the render method to define and render a view template as well as to pass any data to the template that will be interpreted and processed. As we can see from the preceding code, this action is rendering the view template called index.html.twig, which is located in the blog directory.

Database

Symfony 2 does not include a database abstraction layer such as Zend\Db, which we looked at previously. By default, SF2 is configured to use Doctrine, a powerful object relational mapper (ORM) library. While we created a model (entity) layer for our ZF2 example, there are entities that already exist in the Symfony demo application. The entity for the blog post example that our indexAction is invoking is located in the AppBundle/ Entity directory and is called Post.php.

In addition to supplying the entity, our demo application also makes use of a repository for the post database table. Repositories in Doctrine allow you to define methods that perform custom queries on your database. In our indexAction, it invokes the PostRepository and queryLatest() method. Let's take a look at the code that makes up this method:

```
public function queryLatest()
{
    return $this->getEntityManager()
        ->createQuery('
            SELECT p
            FROM AppBundle:Post p
            WHERE p.publishedAt <= :now
            ORDER BY p.publishedAt DESC
        ')
        ->setParameter('now', new \DateTime())
    ;
}
```

This method makes use of the Doctrine Query Language (DQL) and is very similar to regular SQL. It is the syntactic equivalent of the following SQL:

```
SELECT p.*
FROM post p
WHERE p.published_at <= NOW()
ORDER BY p.published_at DESC
```

This particular code returns a Doctrine Entity Manager object that contains the post data sorted in descending order by the published date. The indexAction makes this query by way of the following code:

```
$query = $this->getDoctrine()->getRepository('AppBundle:Post')-
>queryLatest();
```

This code gets the Doctrine object, loads the Post repository located in the AppBundle, and finally calls the preceding queryLatest() method. This will then be handed off to another library the demo application uses to provide result pagination, and finally the application passes the post data variable to the Twig template by using this line:

```
return $this->render('blog/index.html.twig', array('posts' => $posts));
```

■ **Tip** ZF2 can also be configured to work with Doctrine as an ORM rather than using the Zend Database Abstraction Library.

View

The view name and folder structure in SF2 generally follows the controller name and action. For the example code we're examining from the demo app, it is as follows:

```
view (folder containing views)
- blog (controller name)
  - index.html.twig (Action name)
```

By default, Symfony uses the Twig template engine. Twig is a light but powerful template language that uses a simple syntax and parses templates into pure PHP files.

■ **Note**   Although pure PHP templates are supported in Symfony, just as with Zend Framework 2, it is being considered that Twig will become the only officially supported template engine with Symfony Framework 3.

Display Results

The final step in our demo application is processing the data that is passed in by the Symfony render method and displaying it in the blog index view template. Let's take a look at the block of code in the template that handles this:

```
{% for post in posts %}
    <article class="post">
        <h2>
            <a href="{{ path('blog_post', { slug: post.slug }) }}">
                {{ post.title }}
            </a>
        </h2>

        {{ post.summary|md2html }}
    </article>
{% else %}
    <div class="well">{{ 'post.no_posts_found'|trans }}</div>
{% endfor %}
```

This code uses the Twig equivalent of a standard PHP foreach, like we used in our ZF2 example. However, the Twig for method has a convention for automatically handling if there is no data available in the post variable by way of an else statement.

Laravel 5

The last of the PHP frameworks that we're going to look at is Laravel. Laravel is one of the newer frameworks but it has quickly risen in popularity within the PHP community for being clean, fast, and easy to work with.

One of the most important features of Laravel is that it is very configurable, extendable, and a very useful Blade template engine. Laravel was created by Taylor Otwell in an attempt to provide an advanced alternative to an aging PHP framework called CodeIgniter. The first beta release of Laravel was in June 2011.

Installing Laravel 5

Just as with the other frameworks, there are a few ways to install Laravel. The recommended way is through Composer. For the purpose of this exercise, we're going to use the Laravel quickstart project along with the Laravel Homestead Vagrant box. Homestead is a fully configured Vagrant box with PHP7 and all the system requirements needed to run Laravel.

First, clone the quickstart project:

```
$ git clone https://github.com/laravel/quickstart-basic laravel
```

Now install all of the dependencies:

```
$ cd laravel
```

```
$ composer install
```

Next, install Homestead. This will give you the tools to generate the Vagrantfile to run the Laravel Homestead box:

```
$ composer require laravel/homestead --dev
```

```
$ php vendor/bin/homestead make
```

Now bring up the new box:

```
$ vagrant up
```

Lastly, ssh into the new box and run the database migration scripts to install the sample database for the Laravel quickstart app:

```
$ vagrant ssh
```

```
$ cd laravel
```

```
$ php artisan migrate
```

The Homestead box is built using settings that are generated in the Homestead.yaml configuration file. If you open this file, you will see the IP defined for this new Vagrant virtual machine. In this case, it is set by default to 192.168.10.10. If you load this site in your browser, you should see the quickstart app page (Figure 5-8).

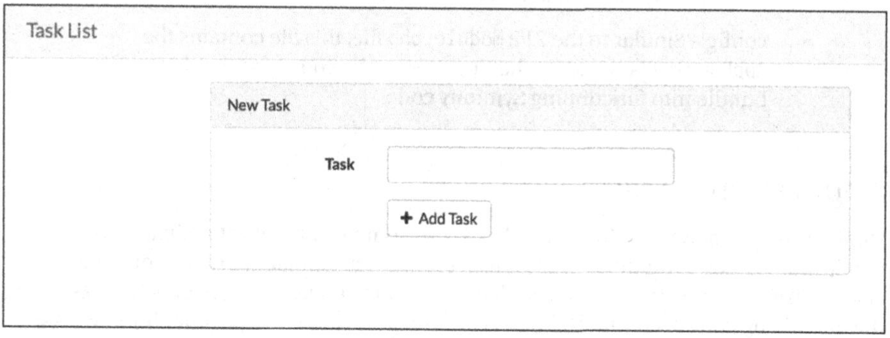

Task List

New Task

Task

+ Add Task

Figure 5-8. The quickstart app page displayed in a browser

Application Directory Structure

If you look into the directory in which you installed the Laravel quickstart project, you will see the various folders that make up a Laravel application (Figure 5-9).

Figure 5-9. The folders that comprise a Laravel application

As with the other frameworks we examined, each directory stores a specific piece of your application. Here is the breakdown of the three most important directories:

- app – This is where all the code lives.

- bootstrap – This serves mostly as the "M" in MVC (model) in that it contains all of the database entities that map the database to code.

- config – Similar to the ZF2 module.php file, this file contains the AppBundle class and is what transforms the code contained in a bundle into functioning Symfony code.

Application Logic

Unlike Zend Framework or Symfony, there is no compartmentalization in a base Laravel application by way of modules or bundles. A somewhat similar approach could be accomplished by creating separate folders under the Laravel app folder and namespacing the underlying code accordingly, but it is not a necessity as with the other frameworks.

Controllers & Routes

In Laravel there are two ways to provide the controller layer of your MVC application. The simplest is by using the app/Http/routes.php file and declaring an anonymous function. This is the approach that is taken for the quickstart application that we're examining, as seen here:

```
Route::get('/', function () {
    return view('tasks', [
        'tasks' => Task::orderBy('created_at', 'asc')->get()
    ]);
});
```

If you wanted to instead move this to a controller, you would add your controller to the app/Http/Controllers directory and define the controller in the routes.php file instead:

```
namespace App\Http\Controllers;

use App\User;
use App\Http\Controllers\Controller;
```

```
class TaskController extends Controller
{
    public function tasks()
    {
        $tasks = Task::orderBy('created_at', 'asc')->get();

        return view('tasks', ['tasks' => $tasks]);
    }
}
```

Now we define the route in routes.php:

```
Route::get('/', TaskController@tasks);
```

This route tells Laravel to use the IndexController and execute the tasks method.

Database

Laravel includes Eloquent, its own ActiveRecord-based implementation of an Object
Relational Mapping (ORM) library, in the base install. Eloquent is touted as being simple
and easy to use. Rather than using entities, as with the previous examples, each database
is represented in one model class. As you can see from the included Task model, the code
needed is very minimal:

```
namespace App;

use Illuminate\Database\Eloquent\Model;

class Task extends Model
{
    //
}
```

By default, Laravel will try to use the plural, lowercase version of a model's class
name for the database table name it is representing. In this example, it would be tasks. It
also expects each table to have a primary key column named id as well as two timestamp
columns called created_at and updated_at. These will get used when all of the tasks are
retrieved in the view.

View

All views in Laravel are stored under the resources/views directory. View templates can
be arranged however desired, such as in sub-directories under this main views directory.
Laravel provides the ability to use either pure PHP-based templates or Blade, a templating
language created by Laravel. The view for the quickstart app is written in Blade and can
be found under resources/views/tasks.blade.php.

Display Results

Let's look again at the anonymous function declared in the routes.php file:

```
return view('tasks', [
        'tasks' => Task::orderBy('created_at', 'asc')->get()
    ]);
```

This uses the get() method with Eloquent to retrieve all tasks ordered by the required created_at column. This is the equivalent of running the following SQL statement:

```
SELECT * FROM tasks ORDER BY created_at ASC
```

Lastly, by calling the view() method and passing it this data, the code hands the data off to the template for use. If we look at the template, we can see the Blade syntax that checks to see if there are any results in the variable $tasks, and, if there are, it loops through them with a foreach loop:

```
<!-- Current Tasks -->
@if (count($tasks) > 0)
<div class="panel panel-default">
    <div class="panel-heading">
        Current Tasks
    </div>

    <div class="panel-body">
        <table class="table table-striped task-table">
            <thead>
            <th>Task</th>
            <th> </th>
            </thead>
            <tbody>
            @foreach ($tasks as $task)
            <tr>
                <td class="table-text">
                    <div>{{ $task->name }}</div>
                </td>

                <!-- Task Delete Button -->
                <td>
                    <form action="/task/{{ $task->id }}" method="POST">
                        {{ csrf_field() }}
                        {{ method_field('DELETE') }}
```

```
                    <button type="submit" class="btn btn-danger">
                        <i class="fa fa-btn fa-trash"></i>Delete
                    </button>
                </form>
            </td>
        </tr>
        @endforeach
        </tbody>
    </table>
</div>
</div>
@endif
```

Micro-Frameworks

Micro-frameworks exist as an alternative for when you want the structure and speed of development provided by a framework, but with fewer "bells and whistles" and less overhead than a traditional full framework provides.

There are many different micro-frameworks available for PHP. Here are a few current popular choices:

- Silex – This is a micro-framework by Sensio Labs and is based on several different Symfony components.

- Lumen – This is a micro-framework by Laravel and is based on some of Laravel's foundations.

- Slim – This is regarded as one of the smallest and fastest PHP micro-frameworks available.

- Phalcon - This is an open source, full-stack framework for PHP and is written as a C-extension.

- Yii - This is an open source, object-oriented, component-based MVC PHP framework.

When to Use a Micro-Framework

There are no hard and fast rules regarding when to use a micro-framework versus a full framework. It is entirely a personal decision and can fluctuate from project to project. As their name implies, micro-frameworks are generally regarded as being for use with small projects, but nothing is preventing you from using it for a project of any size. As with any framework, you need to carefully weigh the scope, size, and functionality of what you are building and make a decision from there. Reading through documentation and features of any given framework, be it micro or full, will give you important insight into what that framework can offer you.

Using a Micro-Framework

So what does developing with a micro-framework look like? Let's dive in and take a look a very simple "hello world" example using three of the frameworks I previously listed. In each of these examples we'll just install the framework and define a simple route and controller to print "hello world".

■ **Tip**   The sample code provided with this book contains a basic Vagrantfile that provides a simple VM on which to run the micro-framework examples.

Silex

To get started with Silex, we first have to install it. Using Composer is the easy and recommended method. To do that, let's create a composer.json file requiring Silex:

```
{
  "require": {
    "silex/silex": "~1.3"
  }
}
```

Now, we run composer install:

```
$ composer install
Loading composer repositories with package information
Installing dependencies (including require-dev)
...
Writing lock file
Generating autoload files
```

That's it–Silex is now set up and ready for our use. To create our extremely simple example, all we need to do is create a single file that includes the Silex autoloader, define the route, execute Silex, and display a simple HTML response. Let's look at the code needed to do this:

```php
<?php

require_once __DIR__.'/../vendor/autoload.php';

// Initialize Silex
$app = new Silex\Application();

// Define a route and anonymous function for our "controller"
$app->get('/hello-world', function () {
    return '<h1>Hello World!</h1>';
});

$app->run();
```

Now, if we visit /hello-world in our browser, we'll see "Hello World!" output onto the screen. Of course, Silex is much more powerful than and capable of more than simple routes and HTML responses. Silex provides a number of other functionality and services available to you with Symfony, including:

- Twig service provider so you can also leverage the power of Twig templates within Silex.

- Dynamic routing

- Database interaction using Doctrine

- Forms, validation, and sessions handling

- Logging, PHPUnit integration, and much more

Lumen

Next up on our list is Lumen. We can install Lumen either by first installing the Lumen installer or by using composer create-project. For our example we'll use composer create-project and run the example on the Laravel Homestead Vagrant box, just as we did with our earlier Laravel example:

```
$ composer create-project --prefer-dist laravel/lumen lumen
Installing laravel/lumen (v5.2.1)
...
Writing lock file
Generating autoload files
```

Now, with Lumen installed, let's add the Homestead Vagrant config:

```
$ composer require laravel/homestead --dev

$ php vendor/bin/homestead make
```

We can now boot our Vagrant box and test out our simple "hello world" example. Just as with Laravel, we define routes under app/Http/routes.php. The syntax to create our example looks almost exactly like that in Silex:

```php
<?php

// Define our hello world route
$app->get('/hello-world', function () {
    return '<h1>Hello World!</h1>';
});
```

As you might notice here, the biggest difference between this and the Silex example is the absence of the autoloader including and executing the run method of Silex. This is because this is all happening in the front-controller defined under `public/index.php`:

```php
<?php

$app = require __DIR__.'/../bootstrap/app.php';

$app->run();
```

As you can see, this is all nearly identical to how the Silex micro-framework is structured. The primary differences between these two are the underlying components of the framework. This should help make your decision between these two frameworks much easier if you already have a preference of Symfony or Laravel.

Slim

Last on our list is Slim. To install Slim, we'll use Composer, just as we did with Silex. We'll create a `composer.json` file then run `composer install`:

```json
{
  "require": {
    "slim/slim": "^3.0"
  }
}
```

```
$ composer install
Loading composer repositories with package information
...
Writing lock file
Generating autoload files
```

Now that Slim is installed, we'll define a single file to which we'll pass our request. This will define the route as well as an anonymous function to perform the "hello world" response:

```php
<?php

use Psr\Http\Message\ServerRequestInterface as Request;
use Psr\Http\Message\ResponseInterface as Response;

// Include Slim autoloader
require_once __DIR__.'/../vendor/autoload.php';

// Initialize Slim
$app = new Slim\App();
```

```
// Define a route and anonymous function to serve as a controller
$app->get('/hello-world', function (Request $request, Response $response) {
    $response->getBody()->write("Hello World!");

    return $response;
});

$app->run();
```

As you can see here, this is again very similar to Silex. We include the Slim autoloader, initialize Slim, define our route and pass in the required Request and Response objects, return our text, and finally execute Slim.

If you look through the source and documentation for Slim, you will quickly notice it is definitely a lot lighter than either Silex or Lumen. It does provide a few add-ons, such as for using Twig templates within your app, but you will notice it's missing some other default functionality that the others provide out of the box, such as database interaction. Although this should be taken into consideration when choosing a micro-framework to use, it should be noted that because of Slim's use of Composer and the modularity that Composer provides, you can quickly and rather easily make use of an ORM such as Doctrine or Laravel's Eloquent.

Summary

In this chapter we covered the benefits provided to you by using a PHP framework, as well as looked at how quickly you could be up and running with some of the most popular full frameworks and micro-frameworks. Even though we only scratched the surface of what it is like to use a framework, hopefully you now have a much better understanding of how they work and are able to start using one in your projects right away.

Index

© Chad Russell 2016
C. Russell, *PHP Development Tool Essentials*, DOI 10.1007/978-1-4842-0683-6

■ S, T, U

■ V, W, X, Y

Get the eBook for only $5!

Why limit yourself?

Now you can take the weightless companion with you wherever you go and access your content on your PC, phone, tablet, or reader.

Since you've purchased this print book, we're happy to offer you the eBook in all 3 formats for just $5.

Convenient and fully searchable, the PDF version enables you to easily find and copy code—or perform examples by quickly toggling between instructions and applications. The MOBI format is ideal for your Kindle, while the ePUB can be utilized on a variety of mobile devices.

To learn more, go to www.apress.com/companion or contact support@apress.com.

Printed in the United States
By Bookmasters